My
Peace-Filled
Day

Shippensburg, PA

A *Sparkling Gems from the Greek*
Guided Devotional Journal

My
Peace-Filled
Day

Rick Renner

Published by Harrison House Publishers
Shippensburg, PA 17257

ISBN 13 TP: 978-1-6675-0247-2

ISBN 13 eBook: 978-1-6675-0248-9

For Worldwide Distribution, Printed in the U.S.A.

1 2 3 4 5 6 7 8 / 27 26 25 24 23

Contents

Preface

Dear Reader,

I put this guided journal together to help you engage the truths of the Bible that I've expounded on in these pages. I understand completely that it's our knowledge of the truth and our *acting* on that truth, making it applicable to our lives, that makes us totally free.

In this devotional journal, I delve into the Greek text to unpack the rich meaning of the words of the New Testament that were written by the inspiration of God. As you press into walking in His peace that surpasses your present circumstances — and the despairing thoughts the enemy uses to trouble your mind — remember this age-abiding truth: *Peace is ALWAYS God's will for you.*

Jesus' own words communicate this truth to all who follow Him as Savior and Lord: "I leave the gift of peace with you — my peace. Not the kind of fragile peace given by the world, but my perfect peace. Don't yield to fear or be troubled in your hearts — instead, be courageous!" (John 14:27 *TPT*).

That is my prayer for you — that as you embrace the truths of the Bible contained in this journal, you will make them your own and experience the gift of this *un-fragile*, *unbreakable* peace in your heart and mind.

Your friend,

Rick Renner
Moscow, Russia

Day 1

Let God's Peace Serve as an Umpire for Your Mind and Emotions!

> *And let the peace of God rule in your hearts, to the which also ye are called in one body; and be ye thankful.*
>
> **— Colossians 3:15**

Have you ever had one of those days when there was so much confusion whirling around your head that you felt like screaming, "STOP"?

From time to time, everyone has that kind of a day. And when you do, your temptation is probably either to get in the flesh and react to someone in an ugly way or to get depressed, go to bed, and forget about it all. However, you know that neither choice will help you solve the problems you are facing.

Rather than throw in the towel and give way to these emotions that want to get the best of you, why not stop right now and make a decision to let the

Word of God rule you today? When I say "rule" you, I'm talking about God's supernatural peace dominating and governing every emotion and situation that confronts you. If you don't make this decision and follow through with it, worry, fear, insecurity, doubt, and a whole host of other emotions will assuredly try to take control. And there is no worse rollercoaster ride than when you are being knocked all over the place by emotions that are out of control!

Instead, let the peace of God rule in your heart, as Paul wrote in Colossians 3:15. He said, "And let the peace of God rule in your hearts, to the which also ye are called in one body; and be ye thankful." I especially want you to notice the word "rule" in this verse. It is from the Greek word *brabeuo*, which in ancient times was used to describe the umpire or referee who moderated and judged the athletic competitions that were so popular in the ancient world.

Paul uses this word to tell us that the peace of God can work like an umpire or referee in our hearts, minds, and emotions. When detrimental emotions attempt to exert control over us or try to throw us into an emotional frenzy, we can stop it from happening by making the choice to let God's peace rise up from deep inside us like an umpire or referee to moderate our emotions. As we do, we will be kept under the control of that divine peace as it rules in our hearts. When this divine umpire called "peace" steps into the game, it suddenly begins to call the shots and make all the decisions instead of fretfulness, anxiety, and worry.

Colossians 3:15 could be translated:

> *"Let the peace of God call the shots in your life...."*
> *"Let the peace of God be the umpire in your life and actions...."*
> *"Let the peace of God act as referee in your emotions and your decisions...."*

Even though it's true that everyone has hard days and difficult weeks, you don't have to surrender to those emotions that try to steal your joy, disturb your relationships, and rob you of your victory. When you feel overwhelmed by problems or emotions that are hitting you from every direction, just stop a moment and deliberately set your heart and mind on Jesus and the Word of God. As you do this, the wonderful, conquering, dominating, supernatural peace of God will rise up from your spirit and take control!

My Prayer for Today

Lord, I don't want to let my emotions get the best of me today, so I ask that Your peace would rise up like a mighty umpire and referee in my heart, mind, and emotions. Help me recognize those moments when unhelpful emotions try to sneak up on me. I ask You to teach me how to put those emotions aside and release Your supernatural peace that is resident in my heart — the peace that is always ready at every moment to moderate every thought and emotion that tries to pass into my life!

I pray this in Jesus' name!

My Confession for Today

I confess that God's supernatural peace dominates me. When I am tempted to get upset, and my emotions try to take control of me, I put these emotions aside and allow the Spirit of God to release a supernatural, dominating, moderating peace to rule my heart, mind, and emotions!

I declare this by faith in Jesus' name!

Questions for You to Consider

1. Do you recognize moments when your emotions try to throw you into an emotional tizzy and steal your peace and joy?

    _____

    _____

    _____

    _____

    _____

    _____

2. Have you asked God to help you overcome these moments?

    _____

    _____

    _____

    _____

    _____

    _____

3. What steps can you take to quiet yourself so you can focus on God's Word and allow the peace of God to rise up and referee what is going on inside your heart, mind, and emotions?

_____

_____

_____

_____

_____

_____

Day 2

Relax From the Stresses of Life!

> *And to you who are troubled rest with us....*
>
> — 2 Thessalonians 1:7

If you have been under a lot of stress, pressure, and anxiety lately, I think Paul's words in Second Thessalonians 1:7 are meant just for you! Read carefully, because you're going to find real encouragement and instruction today that will help you find peace in the midst of trouble.

When Paul wrote the book of Second Thessalonians, the believers in the city of Thessalonica were undergoing horrifying persecution. The persecution in this city was worse than it was in other places because Christians were being hunted both by pagan idol worshipers and by unbelieving Jews who detested the Gospel message. As a result of these threatening conditions, members of the Thessalonian church were suffering, and some even paid the price of dying for the Gospel. However, in spite of these afflictions and pressures from outside forces, this congregation refused to surrender to defeat.

When Paul addressed these believers in Second Thessalonians, they had already been under this stress and pressure for a long period of time. The assaults against them had been like a stream of unrelenting poundings from which they had no pause. Naturally, they were exhausted — extremely tired, worn out, and fatigued. It had been a very long time since they had put up their feet and taken a break! The idea of unwinding or lightening up almost seemed like a fantasy. But everyone needs to rest at some point!

If you've been going through a prolonged period of hardship due to persecution, your business, your family, your relationships, your finances, or your children, you still must learn how to rest in the Lord, even in the middle of that difficult situation you are facing. If you don't, the battle will wear you out!

That's why Paul told the Thessalonians, "And to you who are troubled rest with us...." The word "troubled" tells us the extent of their hardships. It is from the Greek word *thlipsis*, a word Paul often employs when he describes difficult events that he and his team have encountered. This word is so strong that it is impossible to misunderstand the intensity of these persecutions. It conveys the idea of a heavy-pressure situation. In fact, one scholar commented that the word *thlipsis* was first used to describe the specific act of tying a victim with a rope, laying him on his back, and then placing a huge boulder on top of him until his body was crushed. As time progressed, this word came to describe any situation that was crushing or debilitating.

One example of this can be found in Second Corinthians 1:8, where Paul writes, "For we would not, brethren, have you ignorant of our trouble which came to us in Asia...." The word "trouble" in this verse is also from the word *thlipsis*. It could be translated, "We would not, brethren, have you ignorant of the horribly tight, life-threatening squeeze that came to us in Asia...." By using this word, Paul lets us know that his time in Asia was one of the most grueling nightmares he had ever undergone. In fact, when he was in the midst of the situation, he didn't even know if he would survive it!

Now, this is exactly the word Paul uses when he writes to the Thessalonian believers and says, "To those of you who are troubled...." The word "troubled" alerts us to the fact that they were not just mildly suffering; they were horrifically suffering — and as noted earlier, this suffering had gone on for a very long time. But because Paul had been in these types of adverse circumstances himself on different occasions and had victoriously survived, he knew that for the Thessalonians to outlast these difficulties, they needed to take a break from the pressure! That is why he told them, "...Rest with us."

The word "rest" comes from the Greek word *anesis*, which means to let up, to relax, to stop being stressed, or to find relief. One scholar comments that the word *anesis* was used in the secular Greek world to denote the release of a bowstring that has been under great pressure. It was also used figuratively to mean relaxation from the stresses of life and freedom to have a little recreation. By using this word, Paul urges the believers in the city of Thessalonica to find relief from the constant stress they are undergoing as a result of opposition to their faith. Paul exhorts them to let it go, shake it off, and learn how to relax, even in the midst of difficult circumstances.

An interpretive translation of this verse could be:

"To you who are still going through difficulties right now, it's time for you to let up, take a breather, and relax. We know what it's like to be under pressure, but no one can stay under that kind of stress continuously. So, join us in learning how to loosen up a bit. Shake off your troubles, and allow yourself a little relaxation and time for recreation...."

I realize that when you're dealing with problems, a vacation is the last thing on your mind! You just want to survive the challenge and make a transition into the next phase of your life — and do it as soon as possible! You may even feel that it's irresponsible for you to put up your feet and relax for a while. But even God rested on the seventh day!

Take Paul's counsel to heart, and allow yourself a little relaxation and time for recreation — time away from your problems. When it's time to come back and face those problems again, you'll be refreshed and recharged with renewed vision. You'll see that challenge with new eyes, and you'll face it with new strength. Yes, I know it's hard to allow yourself the time to do what I'm suggesting. But, friend, your survival depends on it. If you don't take a break from that constant stress, it will keep wearing you down until you become easy prey for the devil.

So, say goodbye to your problems today. Take a break, and allow yourself a little time to rest, relax, and recuperate!

My Prayer for Today

Lord, I admit that I've been carrying the worries, stresses, and pressures of life for too long. Before I do anything else, I want to cast these burdens over onto You today. I am tempted to worry that the problems I'm facing won't work out, but taking them into my own hands and worrying about them isn't going to make the situation any better. So, I repent for letting myself become consumed with worry about things I cannot change, and I turn them all over to You today. Please help me stay free of anxiety as I learn to relax and enjoy life a little more than I've been enjoying it lately!

I pray this in Jesus' name!

My Confession for Today

I confess that I need to set aside time for relaxation and recreation. Starting today, I'm going to take a break from my problems. I am casting my burdens on the Lord; as a result, I know I will be refreshed, recharged, and given a renewed vision. After a little rest, I will see my challenge with new eyes, and I'll face it with new strength. I know my survival depends on this, so today I choose to take a break from the constant stress I've been dealing with before I get worn down and become easy prey for the devil. God will give me the strength and energy I need to get up and get going so I can complete the work He has entrusted into my hands.

I declare this by faith in Jesus' name!

Questions for You to Consider

1. When was the last time you took some time to rest and relax from the pressures in your life?

   _____

   _____

   _____

   _____

   _____

   _____

2. What are some signs in your life that you need to take time to rest and gain a fresh perspective about the situations you're facing right now?

   _____

   _____

   _____

   _____

   _____

   _____

3. What are some of the best ways you've discovered that help you rest and recuperate during a stressful time in your life?

_____

_____

_____

_____

_____

_____

Day 3

Are You Wearing Your Killer Shoes?

> *Stand therefore, having your loins girt about with truth, and having on the breastplate of righteousness; and your feet shod with the preparation of the gospel of peace....*
>
> — Ephesians 6:14,15

If you had seen the shoes of a Roman soldier, you'd have wanted to make sure you didn't fall in front of him or get in his way where he might accidentally step on you. Those weren't normal shoes — they were killer shoes!

Paul refers to these killer shoes in Ephesians 6:15 as he talks about the spiritual weapons God has given to the Church. Just as God has given each believer a sword, He has also clothed every believer with the shoes of peace.

Now, I realize that these shoes may sound like a passive, peaceful part of our spiritual armor. However, these are actually killer shoes, such as those worn by a Roman soldier.

The shoes of a Roman soldier were vicious weapons. They began at the top of the legs near the knees and extended down to the feet. The portions that covered the knees to the feet were called the "greaves." They were made of metal and were specially shaped to wrap around the calves of a soldier's legs. The greaves were uncomfortable but essential for the safekeeping of a soldier's legs.

The shoe itself was made of heavy pieces of leather or metal tied together with leather straps that were intermingled with bits of metal. The bottoms were manufactured of heavy leather or pieces of metal. The bottom of the shoes were affixed with sharp, dangerous, protruding spikes. These spikes had several purposes, which we will get to in just a moment. In addition, two sharply pointed spikes extended beyond the front of each shoe.

Let me explain to you the reasons for all this gear on a soldier's legs and feet. First, the greaves — the metal that covered the Roman soldier's legs from his knees to the top of his feet — were designed to protect the soldier's calves when he was required to march through rocky and thorny terrain. If he'd had no protection on his legs, he would have surely been gashed and cut by the environment.

Thus, the greaves gave the soldier protection so he could keep walking, regardless of the obstacles he encountered. The metal barriers also gave him defensive protection in those moments when an adversary kicked him in the shins, trying to break his legs. Because the soldier's calves were covered with these greaves, his legs could not be broken, and the enemy's attacks were in vain.

Now let's talk about the spikes on the bottom of the soldier's shoes. These were intended to hold him "in place" when in battle. His opponent might try to push him around, but the spikes on the bottom of his shoes helped keep him in his place, making the soldier virtually immovable. Additionally, those spikes on the bottom and front of the shoes served as weapons of brutality and murder. One good kick with those shoes, and an enemy would be dead. Just a few seconds of stomping on a fallen adversary would have eradicated that foe forever!

When Paul writes about these shoes in Ephesians 6:15, he says, "...And your feet shod with the preparation of the gospel of peace." Notice that he connects peace with these killer weapons! In just a moment, you'll understand why.

The word "shod" is derived from the word *hupodeomai* — a compound of the words *hupo* and *deo*. The word *hupo* means under, and *deo* means to bind. Taken together as one word, it conveys the idea of binding something very tightly on the bottom of one's feet. Therefore, this is not the picture of a loosely fitting shoe but of a shoe that has been tied onto the bottom of the foot extremely tightly.

Just as the greaves of a Roman soldier protected him from the environment and from the blows of his enemy, the peace of God — when it is operating in your life — protects and defends you from the hassles and assaults of the devil. The enemy may try to disrupt you, distract you, and steal your attention by causing negative events to whirl all around you, but his attempts will fail because the peace of God, like a protective greave, stops you from being hurt and enables you to keep marching forward!

Just as those spikes held a Roman soldier securely in place when his enemy tried to push him around, the peace of God will hold you in place when the devil tries to push you around! And as the soldier used those spikes to kick and to kill his opponent, there is no need for you to ever stop moving ahead just because the devil tries to block your path. If he is foolish enough to try to get in front of you, just keep walking! Stomp all along the way! By the time you're finished using your shoes of peace, you won't have much of a devil problem to deal with anymore!

Paul uses this illustration to tell us that we must firmly tie God's peace onto our lives. If we only give peace a loosely fitting position in our lives, it won't be long before the affairs of life knock our peace out of place. Hence, we must bind peace onto our minds and emotions in the same way Roman soldiers made sure to bind their shoes very tightly onto their feet.

But wait — there's one more important point. Paul continued, "And your feet shod with the preparation...." The word "preparation" is the Greek word *etoimasin*, and it presents the idea of readiness or preparation. When used in connection with Roman soldiers, the word *etoimasin* portrayed men of war who had their shoes tied on very tightly to ensure a firm footing. Once they had the assurance that their shoes were going to stay in place, they were ready to march out onto the battlefield and confront the enemy.

When peace is in place in your life, it gives you the assurance you need to step out in faith and make the moves God is leading you to make. But before you take those steps, you need to be sure His peace is operating in your life. This mighty and powerful piece of your spiritual weaponry is essential because, without it, the devil can try to kick, punch, pull, and distract you. But with that conquering peace firmly tied to your mind and emotions, you will be empowered to keep marching ahead, impervious to the devil's attempts to take you down!

My Prayer for Today

Lord, I thank You for the peace You have placed in my life. This powerful spiritual weapon protects me from the assaults of life, enabling me to stand fixed, even in the face of the occasional storms that try to blow into my life, my family, my church, my friendships, and my business. How can I ever express how much I need this peace or how grateful I am to You for covering me with this protective shield that fortifies me and makes me strong? When adverse situations arise against me, help me remember to immediately release this divine force to safeguard my life.

I pray this in Jesus' name!

My Confession for Today

I confess that God's peace rules my mind and emotions, protecting me from the ups and downs of life. When storms are trying to rage against me and situations are hostile toward me, God's peace covers and safeguards me from all harm. Because divine peace is operating in me, I am not easily moved, quickly shaken, or terrified by any events that occur around me. This mighty and powerful piece of spiritual weaponry is mine to use day and night. Therefore, although the devil may try to kick, punch, pull, and distract me, that conquering peace empowers me to keep marching ahead, oblivious to the devil's attempts to take me down!

I declare this by faith in Jesus' name!

Questions for You to Consider

1. Have there been some very difficult times in your life when the peace of God protected you from the turmoil that was happening around you?

   _____

   _____

   _____

   _____

   _____

   _____

2. Do you recall how you felt when you were enveloped in this supernatural peace? Think about it.

   _____

   _____

   _____

   _____

   _____

   _____

3. If the devil is trying to shove you around emotionally right now, what can you do to stay in the peace of God?

_____

_____

_____

_____

_____

Day 4

Peace That Passes Understanding

> *And the peace of God, which passeth all understanding, shall keep your hearts and minds through Christ Jesus.*
>
> — **Philippians 4:7**

Are you tired of letting the devil get you all stirred up? Has it been easy for the enemy to throw you into a frenzy of panic and anxiety? Maybe it doesn't happen continually to you, but every once in a while, something happens, or someone says something that pushes a button inside you and throws you into a tizzy! When this occurs, do you say and do things you later regret? Do you feel sorry that you allowed the devil to get to you again?

If what I just described sounds familiar, I have help for you today! In Philippians 4:7, the apostle Paul writes, "And the peace of God, which passeth all understanding, shall keep your hearts and minds through Christ Jesus."

As we begin our study today, I want to draw your attention to the word "passeth" in the verse above. It is the Greek word *huperecho*, which is a compound of the words *huper* and *echo*. The word *huper* literally means over, above, and beyond. It depicts something that is way beyond measure. It carries the idea of superiority; something that is utmost, paramount, foremost, first-rate, first-class, and topnotch; greater, higher, and better than; superior to; preeminent, dominant, and incomparable; more than a match for; unsurpassed or unequaled. The second part of the word "passeth" is the Greek word *echo*, which means I have, as someone who holds something in his possession. It can be translated to keep; to possess; to have; to hold; or even to acquire.

When these words are compounded into one, they form the word *huperecho*, which Paul uses in Philippians 4:7. This Greek word denotes a peace so superior that it is held high above all other types of peace. This is a peace that transcends, outdoes, surpasses, excels, rises above, and goes beyond and over the top of any other kind of peace. The implication is that people may try to find peace in other places, but there is no peace like the peace of God. The peace of God completely outshines every other attempt to produce peace, causing it to stand in a category by itself. There is absolutely nothing in the world that can compare with the peace of God.

Paul continues to tell us that this peace surpasses and excels above "all understanding." The word "understanding" is the Greek word *nous*, the classical Greek word for the mind. This word refers to the ability to think; to reason; to understand; and to comprehend. It also depicts the mind as the source of all human emotions. In Greek, the word "mind" represents the inner powers of a person and, thus, the place from which a person rules and controls his environment and the world around him. The Greek word emphatically depicts the mind as the central control center for a human being. Therefore, it is understood that the condition of the mind is what determines the condition of one's life.

Then Paul tells us what this powerful peace will produce in our lives! He says that this peace "...shall keep your hearts and minds...." The word "keep" is the Greek word *phroureo*, a military term that expresses the idea of soldiers who stood faithfully at their post at the city gates to guard and control all who went in and out of the city. They served as gate monitors, and no one entered or exited the city without their approval.

The apostle Paul uses this word *phroureo* to explicitly tell us that God's peace, if allowed to work in our lives, will stand at the gates of our hearts and minds, acting like a guard to control and monitor everything that tries to enter our hearts, minds, and emotions. When God's peace is ruling us, nothing can get past that divine "guard" and slip into our hearts and minds without its approval!

This is the good news you've been waiting for! It means you can refuse to allow the devil to access you, throw you into a state of panic and anxiety, or push any button inside you any longer. When the peace of God is standing guard at the entrance of your heart and mind, the devil has lost his access to your thought life and your emotions!

Taking these Greek words together, Philippians 4:7 could be understood in the following way:

> *"And the peace of God — a peace so wonderful that it cannot be compared to any other type of peace; a peace that stands in a category by itself and rises far above and goes beyond anything the human mind could ever think, reason, imagine, or produce by itself — will stand at the entrance of your heart and mind, working like a guard to control, monitor, and screen everything that tries to access your mind, heart, and emotions."*

By using this word, Paul tells us that the peace of God will keep and guard your heart and mind! God's peace will surround your heart and mind just as a band of Roman soldiers would keep dangerous nuisances from entering a city or from breaking into special, private places. In the same way, peace keeps fretfulness, anxiety, worry, and all the other wiles of the devil from breaking into your life. When this peace is active in your life, it surpasses all natural understanding. It protects, guards, keeps, and defends you.

Nothing compares to this powerful, protective, guarding peace that God has positioned to stand at the entrance of your heart and mind! When this peace operates in you, it dominates your mind and your life. Since what's inside you is what rules you, peace rises up and conquers your entire being. It stands at the gate of your heart and mind, disabling the devil's ability to disturb you by preventing his attacks from bypassing and slipping into your mind. The devil may try his best to find access to your mind and emotions, but this guarding peace will paralyze his efforts.

So, make sure Philippians 4:7 is a reality in your life. In every situation you face today and every day, let God's supernatural peace rise up to dominate your heart and protect your mind and emotions. If you're tired of the devil getting you all stirred up and throwing you into a tizzy, it's time for you to let this supernatural peace go to work and start monitoring, guarding, and approving what does and does not get access to you!

My Prayer for Today

Lord, I thank You for placing Your wonderful, powerful, protective peace in my life. I am grateful that You have positioned it to stand at the entrance of my heart and mind and that it dominates my mind and controls my life. Because what is inside me is what rules me, I choose to let this peace rise up and conquer me. With this peace standing at the gate of my heart and mind, I know it will disable the devil's ability to attack my emotions and will not permit his lies and accusations to slip into my mind! Thank You for loving me enough to put this powerful peace in my life!

I pray this in Jesus' name!

My Confession for Today

I confess that I am guarded and protected by the powerful peace of God that works in my life. It rises up to dominate my mind; it controls my thinking; and it determines the condition of my life and the environment where I live and work. I am unaffected by the circumstances that surround me, for this supernatural peace stands at the gate of my mind and emotions to monitor everything that tries to access me. Because no fretting, anxiety, panic, or worry is allowed to enter me, I remain free, calm, and peaceful — even in difficult situations that in the past would have upset me!

I declare this by faith in Jesus' name!

Questions for You to Consider

1. Have you noticed specific events or moments in your life when the devil seems to be able to access your mind and emotions to upset your peace and throw you into one of these regrettable fits I've described to you today? If your answer is yes, do you know the "buttons" he pushes to throw you into this state that you detest?

   _____

   _____

   _____

   _____

   _____

   _____

2. What can you do to slow your reactions down long enough to let the peace of God rise up and conquer your emotions so you don't end up saying and doing things you later regret?

   _____

   _____

   _____

   _____

   _____

3. Why don't you really think this through and ask the Holy Spirit to help you come up with some ideas you can write down and pray about?

_____

_____

_____

_____

_____

_____

Day 5

Joy and Peace

> *But the fruit of the Spirit is love, joy, peace....*
>
> **— Galatians 5:22**

I'll never forget many years ago when a so-called "brother in the Lord" tried to destroy our ministry in the former USSR. When I finally discovered the destructive schemes he was covertly planning, I was dumbfounded — stunned that someone I had worked with so closely could be deviously used by the devil. It was a true "Judas Iscariot" situation.

Thanks to God's Spirit alerting us to what was happening and to staff members who sensed something was wrong in the Spirit, we probed into this man's activities and discovered what he was attempting to do. Soon I found myself on an airplane with several key members of my team, flying to another city to deal with the consequences of his dishonest, deceitful, fraudulent plans.

As we flew that day to an encounter with evil that is forever etched in my memory, my staff commented on how joyful I was in the midst of this potentially devastating situation. I must admit, even I was amazed at the joy that exuded from down deep inside me that day! I knew the joy I felt was being produced in me by the Holy Spirit, for only the Holy Spirit could give such joy in a situation as difficult as the one I was facing that day.

That experience reminded me of Paul's words to the Thessalonians in First Thessalonians 1:6. He told them, "And ye became followers of us, and of the Lord, having received the word in much affliction, with joy of the Holy Ghost." In most of Paul's writings, he associates "joy" with times of affliction. The word "affliction" used in this verse is the Greek word *thlipsis*. This word is so strong that it leaves no room for misunderstanding regarding the intensity of the afflictions the Thessalonians faced.

The word *thlipsis* conveys the idea of a heavy-pressure situation. One scholar says it was first used to describe the specific act of tying a victim with a rope, laying him on his back, and then placing a huge boulder on top of him until his body was crushed. Paul uses this word to alert us to moments when he or others went through grueling, crushing situations that would have been unbearable, intolerable, and impossible to survive if it had not been for the help of the Holy Spirit.

Joy:

One of the ways the Holy Spirit helps in these situations is to give us supernatural "joy." However, it's important to understand that this divine joy isn't on the same low level as mere happiness. Happiness is based on circumstantial pleasure, merriment, hilarity, exuberance, excitement, or something that causes one to feel hopeful or to be in high spirits. These fleeting emotions of happiness, although very pleasurable at the moment, usually go just as quickly as they came. All it takes is one piece of bad news, a sour look from a fellow employee, a harsh word from a spouse, or an electric bill that is larger than what was anticipated — and that emotion of happiness can disappear right before a person's eyes! But joy is unaffected by outward circumstances. In fact, it usually thrives best when times are tough! It is God's supernatural response to the devil's attacks!

The Greek word for "joy" is *chara*, derived from the word *charis*, which is the Greek word for grace. This is important to note, for it tells us categorically that *chara* ("joy") is produced by the *charis* ("grace") of God. This means "joy" isn't a human-based happiness that comes and goes. Rather, true "joy" is divine in origin, a fruit of the Spirit that is manifested particularly in hard times. Someone may feel happiness, merriment, hilarity, exuberance, excitement, or "high spirits," but all of these are fleeting emotions. On the other hand, "joy" is a Spirit-given expression that flourishes best when times are strenuous, daunting, and tough!

In the example given in First Thessalonians 1:6, the Thessalonians were under great stress due to persecution; yet in the midst of it all, they continued to experience great joy. In fact, the Greek strongly implies that their supernatural joy was due to the Holy Spirit working inside them. Paul even called it the "joy of the Holy Ghost."

An interpretive translation of First Thessalonians 1:6 could be the following:

> *"You threw your arms open wide and gladly welcomed the Word into your lives with great enthusiasm. And you did it even in the midst of mind-boggling sufferings — a level of stress and intensity that would be suffocating and crushing for most people. But while you were going through all these hardships and hassles, you were simultaneously experiencing the supreme ecstasy and joy of the Holy Spirit."*

The best that the lost world has to offer is a temporary happiness. But when the seed of God has been placed inside your human spirit, that divine seed produces a "joy" that isn't based on outward events or circumstances. In fact, when times get very challenging, the supernatural life of God rises up inside you to defy that devilish pressure! This supernatural "joy" will sustain you in even the hardest of times!

Peace:

On the day when we faced that difficult ordeal with the man who was trying to destroy our ministry, there was something else I couldn't help but notice: Supernatural "peace" was ruling me and my emotions! Under such circumstances, most people would have been very upset, but I was completely controlled, level-headed, and at rest. My fellow associates kept asking me, "How can you be so peaceful in the midst of this situation?" It was simply a fact that supernatural peace had risen up from deep within my spirit, enabling me to be a rock in the middle of a terrible storm that was threatening to disrupt the outreach of our ministry.

I knew this "peace" wasn't something I was producing by myself; it was a fruit that the Holy Spirit was producing in me. Paul listed this supernatural "peace" in Galatians 5:22 when he wrote about the fruit of the Spirit. He said, "But the fruit of the Spirit is love, joy, peace...."

The word "peace" comes from the Greek word *eirene*, the Greek equivalent of the Hebrew word *shalom*, which expresses the idea of wholeness, completeness, or tranquility in the soul that is unaffected by outward circumstances or pressures. The word *eirene* strongly suggests the rule of order in place of chaos. When a person is dominated by *eirene* ("peace"), he has a calm, inner stability that results in the ability to conduct himself peacefully, even in the midst of circumstances that would normally be very nerve-racking, traumatic, or upsetting.

The Hebrew counterpart, the word *shalom*, indicates that this dominating peace ultimately gives rise to prosperity in one's soul. Rather than allowing the difficulties and pressures of life to break him, a person who is possessed by *eirene* ("peace") is whole, complete, orderly, stable, and poised for blessing.

The New Testament is filled with examples of this supernatural peace that the Holy Spirit produces. One classic example is found in Acts 27 when the apostle Paul found himself in a ship that was being dangerously tossed back and forth by the raging waves of the sea. In fact, the storm was so severe that Acts 27:14 and 15 says, "But not long after there arose against it a tempestuous wind, called Euroclydon. And when the ship was caught, and could not bear up into the wind, we let her drive."

Notice verse 14 says, "...There arose against it a tempestuous wind...." The word "against" is the Greek word *ballo*, which in this verse means to throw, to dash, to hurt, or to rush. It indicates that a massive, terrible force of wind had come against them. He continues to say it was a "tempestuous wind," which is the Greek word *tuphonikos*, a compound of the words *tuphos* and *nikos*. The word *tuphos* means typhoon, and *nikos* means to subdue or to conquer. Put these two words together, and it pictures a typhoon from which there is no escape. This is a storm so immense that it conquers and dominates everything in sight. Acts 27:14 tells us that this storm was called "Euroclydon" — the term professional sailors used to describe the deadly northeastern winter storms that blew across the Mediterranean Sea, causing many shipwrecks that resulted in the loss of many lives every year.

This typhoon became so fierce that Acts 27:15 says, "...The ship was caught, and could not bear up into the wind...." The word "caught" is the Greek word *sunarpadzo*, which means to seize violently or to seize and to carry away. This word lets us know that the sailors had lost control of the ship. The winds were so violent that they could no longer fight them. One scholar noted that it must have felt as if a monster had seized the ship and was tearing it to pieces. The situation was so completely out of the sailors' control that they "let her drive." In other words, they chose to let the storm take them where it wanted rather than try to fight the winds that could not be conquered. Their hope was that the winds would carry them into the smoother waters near the small island of Clauda, which was a mere twenty-three miles south of Crete.

Acts 27:17 tells us that, once in the smooth waters off the shores of Clauda, the crew had much-needed repair work to do before they could continue on their dangerous journey in the winter storm. The ship had sustained a substantial amount of damage because of the fierce winds already endured on this trip. Verse 17 describes the work they undertook to prepare for the rest of the dangerous, windy trip: "Which when they had taken up, they used helps, undergirding the ship; and, fearing lest they should fall into the quicksands, strake sail, and so were driven."

The words "when they had taken up" are from the Greek word *boetheia*, which referred to the ropes or cables used to secure the ship in one location. Before work on the ship could commence, the ship first had to be securely tied in one spot. Once it had been secured, the crew began to repair and prepare the ship for the rest of its hazardous journey.

But notice that this verse also mentions "quicksands," which is from the Greek word *syrtis*, meaning terror. This referred to the sandbars that were located off the coast of North Africa. The fact that these professional sailors feared these sandbars, which were located four hundred miles south of their location at the island of Clauda, tells us that the winds they were fighting were strong enough to take them that far off their navigational course. Ships were constantly wrecked as a result of these sandbars, which were widely known to be the graveyard of countless sailors.

After all the crew's efforts to fix the ship and try to avoid the winter winds, Acts 27:18 continues to tell us, "And we being exceedingly tossed with a tempest, the next day they lightened the ship." The word "exceedingly" is from the word *sphrodros*, which means vehemently, violently, or intensely. The word "tempest" is the Greek word *cheimadzoamai*, which is the Greek word for a storm. But when you put these two words together into one phrase, as in this verse, it pictures a very vehement, violent, and intense storm.

In other words, rather than escaping the storm, the crew must have felt like they were driving right into it! It was such a serious situation that Acts 27:20 says, "And when neither sun nor stars in many days appeared, and no small tempest lay on us, all hope that we should be saved was then taken away."

But right in the midst of all this hopelessness, Paul stood up and said, "And now I exhort you to be of good cheer: for there shall be no loss of any man's life among you, but of the ship. For there stood by me this night the angel of God, whose I am, and whom I serve, saying, Fear not..." (Acts 27:22-24). Paul had heard from the Lord, which caused supernatural peace to rise up on the inside of him. Therefore, he was able to be a rock in the middle of a very serious situation. His peace brought strength to everyone on that ship!

As noted earlier, this kind of "peace" is produced by the Holy Spirit. Now think back on the meaning of the word *eirene* ("peace") in light of Paul's experience on that ship. Remember, this word expresses the idea of wholeness, completeness, or tranquility in the soul that is unaffected by outward circumstances or pressures. It strongly suggests the rule of order in the place of chaos. When a person is dominated by *eirene* ("peace"), he has a calm, inner stability that results in the ability to conduct himself peacefully, even though circumstances normally would be very nerve-racking, traumatic, or upsetting. Isn't this the exact quality Paul manifested that day on the ship?

I know this supernatural peace of the Holy Spirit is what was working in me the day we were facing such difficulties because of that so-called brother in the Lord. That same peace has worked in me in many other difficult situations — and it will work in me many times more in the days that lie ahead!

So don't think you have to give way to upsetting emotions in difficult or challenging moments. If you'll let the Holy Spirit work in you, He will release a supernatural joy and a dominating peace from way down deep inside you. These fruits of the Spirit have the power to keep you joyful, calm, stable, and peaceful, even though you are facing circumstances that would normally push you over the edge! Why don't you take a few minutes today to pray and ask the Holy Spirit to produce the supernatural fruits of joy and peace in you?

My Prayer for Today

Lord, I am so thankful today that You haven't abandoned me to my flesh and my emotions! Because Your Spirit lives in me, I can be empowered to walk in joy and peace in any situation. Forgive me for pandering to the whims of my flesh and for allowing it to rant and rave when Your Spirit inside me is longing to cause His supernatural joy and peace to rule my life. I turn from my past habits of worry and fear, and I deliberately choose to let the Holy Spirit flood me with Your unquenchable joy and incomprehensible peace!

I pray this in Jesus' name!

My Confession for Today

I confess that I am dominated by the fruits of joy and peace. Fear and anxiety have no place in my life; neither am I ruled by the temporary, fleeting emotions of happiness. Joy strengthens me and stabilizes me in every situation. Peace rules my emotions, helping me to maintain stability and eradicate emotional chaos from my life and surroundings. I am inhabited by the Spirit of God Himself — and as I yield to Him, He is controlling me more and more!

I declare this by faith in Jesus' name!

Questions for You to Consider

1. Can you think of a time in your life when you should have been very upset about something, but a supernatural joy came rising up out of your spirit that sustained you during that hard time?

_____

_____

_____

_____

_____

_____

2. Can you also recollect a moment when the peace of God replaced the fear and worry that normally would have conquered you? What do you think would have happened that day if you hadn't been ruled by this supernatural peace?

_____

_____

_____

_____

_____

_____

3. Do you think you have anything to do with the fruits of joy and peace operating in your life? Can your words or actions either stop them from functioning or release them to function more freely in your life?

_____

_____

_____

_____

_____

_____

Day 6

Make Up Your Mind to Live Fearlessly and Peacefully in These Last Days!

> *That ye be not soon shaken in mind, or be troubled, neither by spirit, nor by word, nor by letter as from us, as that the day of Christ is at hand.*
>
> — **2 Thessalonians 2:2**

In Second Thessalonians 2:2, the apostle Paul wrote to the Thessalonian believers and warned them about events that would occur right before the coming of the Lord. He wanted to prepare them so these major world events wouldn't take them off guard and throw them into a state of panic. Therefore, Paul told them, "That ye be not soon shaken in mind, or be troubled, neither by spirit, nor by word, nor by letter as from us, as that the day of Christ is at hand" (2 Thessalonians 2:2).

Notice that Paul told the Thessalonian believers not to be "soon shaken." The word "soon" is the Greek word *tachus*, which means quickly, suddenly, or hastily. The word "shaken" is the Greek word *saleuo*, which means to shake, to waver, to totter, or to be moved. The tense used in the Greek points to events so dramatic that they could result in shock or alarm. In fact, the Greek tense strongly suggests a devastating occurrence or a sequence of devastating occurrences so dramatic that they will throw the world into a state of shock or distress.

By using the words "soon shaken," Paul was urging his readers (and us!) to resist being easily shaken up by events that will occur just before the coming of Jesus. He was particularly careful to mention that we must not be "soon shaken in mind." The Greek word for the "mind" is *nous*, which describes everything in the realm of the intellect, including one's will, emotions, and ability to think, reason, and decide.

Whoever or whatever controls a person's mind ultimately has the power to dictate the affairs and outcome of that person's life. Thus, if a person allows his mind to be doused with panic or fear, he is putting fear in charge of his life. Because Paul wanted his readers to remain in peace regardless of the tumultuous events that transpired around them, he urged them not to allow fear from these shocking and distressful events to penetrate their minds, will, and emotions.

Then to make certain we comprehend the magnitude of these last-day events, Paul went on to say, "That ye be not soon shaken in mind, or be troubled...." The word "troubled" is the Greek word *throeo*, which indicates an inward fright that results from the shocking occurrence described above. The shock resulting from these nerve-racking events could be so severe that it could cause a person to be devoured with worry, anxiety, or fear.

Paul is confident these events will not be only a one-time occurrence; thus, he uses a Greek tense that points to an ongoing state of worry and inward anxiety resulting from these outward events that keep occurring again and again. It is as if he prophesies that there is no pause between these shocking, debilitating, and nerve-racking happenings. One scholar, therefore, translates the word "troubled" as being jumpy or nervous.

These words are so jammed-packed with meaning that it is almost impossible to directly translate them. To help you see exactly what Paul was communicating to his readers, I have translated and paraphrased the original Greek words, pulling the full meaning out of each word and then transferring those meanings into the interpretive translation below.

All the words Paul used in Second Thessalonians 2:2 convey this idea:

> *"Some things will be happening right before His coming that could shake you up quite a bit. I'm referring to events that will be so dramatic that they could really leave your head spinning — occurrences of such a serious nature that many people will end up feeling alarmed, panicked, intimidated, and even unnerved! Naturally speaking, these events could nearly drive you over the brink emotionally, putting your nerves on edge and making you feel apprehensive and insecure about life. I wish I could tell you these incidents were going to be just a one-shot deal, but when they finally get rolling, they're going to keep coming and coming, one after another. That's why you have to determine not to be shaken or moved by anything you see or hear. You need to get a grip on your mind and refuse to allow yourselves to be traumatized by these events. If you let these things get to you, it won't be too long until you're a nervous wreck! So decide beforehand that you are not going to give in and allow 'fright' to worm its way into your mind and emotions until it runs your whole life."*

Paul strongly urges us not to allow ourselves to be shaken or moved by anything we see or hear. He tells us that we must get a grip on our minds and refuse to allow ourselves to be traumatized by the events that occur in the world around us or to allow fear to control our whole lives. Instead of letting these things "get to us" and rob us of our joy, peace, and victory, we need to be deeply rooted in the confidence of God's promises!

If you take a look at the world around us today, it is clear that Paul's prophecy about the last days is unfolding before our very eyes. Because of the many different situations that our generation is facing, we must take a stand against fear and determine to stay in faith! But in order for us to stay in faith, it is imperative that we keep our minds focused on the Word of God.

Colossians 3:15 says, "And let the peace of God rule in your hearts...." Verse 16 goes on to say, "Let the word of Christ dwell in you richly...." When the Word of God dwells richly in our lives, it produces peace — so much supernatural peace that it actually rules our hearts!

The word "rule" that is used in this verse is the Greek word *brabeuo*, which describes an umpire who calls all the shots and makes all the decisions. You see, when God's Word is dwelling richly in your heart, suddenly, the peace of God makes all the big decisions, calls all the shots, and umpires your emotions. Rather than being led by the ups and downs of the day or by what you read in the newspaper, you will be ruled by the wonderful peace of God!

But to receive this benefit of God's Word, you must let it dwell in you richly. This word richly is the Greek word *plousios*, and it can be translated lavishly. This presents the picture of you giving the Word of God a wonderful reception as you roll out the red carpet so you can richly and lavishly welcome the Word into your heart. When you let God's Word have this place of honor inside your heart, mind, and emotions, it releases its power to stabilize you and keep you in peace, even in the most difficult times.

There is no doubt that we are living in the very end of the last days. We are a chosen generation — and we will observe events that no other generation has ever seen.

If you are going to keep your heart fear-free so you can live in continual peace, you must make a firm commitment to let God's Word rule in your heart! God's Word will protect your mind and prohibit fear from worming its way into your emotions and turning you into an emotional mess. Is God's Word the foundation of your life today?

My Prayer for Today

Lord, I am so thankful that Your Word prepares us for every event that comes along in this life! I know I am living in the last days and that these challenging times require a higher level of commitment from me if I am going to live free from fear. This is such a critical moment for me to be strong, free, and secure. When I am strong, I can be a tower of strength to others who are drowning in the world around me. Help me be that source of strength and power to the people who surround me, Lord. I want to be all that I need to be in this hour.

I pray this in Jesus' name!

My Confession for Today

I confess that God's Word dominates my mind, my will, and my emotions! Because I have put God's Word into my heart, I am not shaken or easily moved by the things that occur in the world around me. I know who I am; I am secure in my Father's love; and I recognize that He destined me to live in these last days because He has a special plan for me. Regardless of what I see or hear, I take my stand on the promises of God's Word, and it provides me with safety and security!

I declare this by faith in Jesus' name!

Questions for You to Consider

1. In light of the world events that have occurred in recent years, how pertinent to you are Paul's words in Second Thessalonians 2:2? Does it sound like Paul is writing about the nonstop traumatic events that have shaken the world over the past several years?

_____

_____

_____

_____

_____

_____

2. If it is true that we are living in the last days just before the coming of Jesus Christ, how should this affect the manner in which you are living your life?

_____

_____

_____

_____

_____

3. Do you spend more time reading your Bible, reading the news-paper, or watching the news? Whatever you dwell on the most is what will dominate you, so isn't it time that you make God's Word the primary focus of your attention?

_____

_____

_____

_____

_____

_____

Day 7

Five Important Steps to Move from Fear to Faith, from Turmoil to Peace, and from Defeat to Victory!

> *Be careful for nothing; but in every thing by prayer and supplication with thanksgiving let your requests be made known unto God.*
>
> **— Philippians 4:6**

I vividly remember a time in my life when I was very concerned about something that was about to occur. Although the challenge before me really wasn't so life-shattering, at the moment, it seemed huge and mountainous. Therefore, I was extremely concerned.

I'm sure you know what it's like when worry tries to flood your mind. It has a way of magnifying issues to the point of being ridiculous, but when you're in the midst of the situation, it seems so real. Only after the event has passed do you realize how silly it was to be so worried about something that was so non-eventful.

But at the time I'm telling you about right now, I was consumed with worry. I paced back and forth, fretting, thinking, and pondering, making myself even more nervous by my anxious behavior. I was nothing but a bag of nerves. Realizing how deeply I was sinking into worry, I reached for my Bible to try to find peace for my troubled soul. I opened it to Philippians 4:6, which says, "Be careful for nothing; but in everything by prayer and supplication with thanksgiving let your requests be made known unto God."

I tried to push everything else out of my mind so I could concentrate on God's words in this verse. Through Philippians 4:6, I could see that God was calling out to me and urging me to lay down my worries and come boldly before Him to make my requests known. As I focused on this verse, I suddenly saw something I had never seen before. I realized that this verse showed me step by step how to lay down my worries and boldly make my requests known to God. If I followed the steps laid out in this verse exactly as I understood them, I would be set free from worry and fear! I promptly followed these steps, and in a matter of minutes, my worry was replaced with a thankful, praising, and peaceful heart!

As the years have passed, I have had many occasions when worry and fear have tried to plague my mind. It would be impossible to exaggerate the challenges my wife and I have faced as we've fulfilled our apostolic ministry overseas. At times, these challenges have simply been enormous.

This is the reason I so entirely identify with the apostle Paul as he describes the difficulties he encountered in his ministry. Just as Satan regularly tried to disrupt Paul's ministry, the enemy has also attempted on many occasions to hinder our work and thwart the advancement of the Gospel. However, none of his attacks have ever succeeded, and the Gospel has gone forth in mighty power!

In moments when worry or fear is trying to wrap its life-draining tentacles around me, I rush back to the truths found in Philippians 4:6. Just as I followed the steps found in this verse so many years ago, I still carefully follow them whenever I start getting anxious. Every time I do, these steps lead me from worry and fear to a thankful, praising, and peaceful heart. In fact, I have learned that if I faithfully follow these steps, fear will always be eradicated and replaced with the wonderful, dominating peace of God.

So don't let worry wrap its tentacles around you. Instead, listen to Paul's advice about how to deal with the problems and concerns that try to assail your mind. Let's look once again at what he says in Philippians 4:6: "Be careful for nothing; but in everything by prayer and supplication with thanksgiving let your requests be made known unto God."

In this verse, Paul lays out five very important steps to move from fear to faith, from turmoil to peace, and from defeat to victory. We'll look at five key words that tell us exactly what we must do when worry and concerns are trying to assail our minds: 1) prayer; 2) supplication; 3) thanksgiving; 4) requests; and 5) known.

When Paul uses the word "prayer" in this verse, it is the Greek word *proseuche*, which is the most commonly used word for prayer in the New Testament. This particular word and its various forms is used approximately 127 times in the New Testament. It is a compound of the words *pros* and *euche*. The word *pros* is a preposition that means toward, which can denote a sense of closeness. Nearly everywhere it is used in the New Testament, the word *pros* carries the meaning of close, up-front, intimate contact with someone else.

One scholar has noted that the word *pros* is used to portray the intimate relationship that exists between the members of the Godhead. John 1:1 says, "In the beginning was the Word, and the Word was with God...." The word "with" is taken from the word *pros*. By using this word to describe the relationship between the Father and the Son, the Holy Spirit is telling us that theirs is an intimate relationship. One expositor has translated the verse, "In the beginning was the Word, and the Word was face-to-face with God...."

The second part of the word *proseuche* is taken from the word *euche*. The word *euche* is an old Greek word that describes a wish, desire, prayer, or vow. It was originally used to depict a person who made some kind of vow to God because of a need or desire in his or her life. This individual would vow to give something of great value to God in exchange for a favorable answer to prayer. Thus, inherent in this word is the idea of an exchange — giving something to God in exchange for something wanted or desired.

So instead of carrying your worries and burdens, you are to take the first step Paul gives you in moving from a place of turmoil to peace: Come close to the Lord in prayer. Once you are in that intimate, face-to-face place with God, take that opportunity to give Him your worries, fears, and concerns. Then ask the Lord to give you something back in exchange for the worries you have given Him — ask Him for peace! You see, this is a part of the great exchange found in the Greek word *proseuche*. When you give God your problems, in return He gives you His peace.

Perhaps you've experienced this great exchange at some previous moment in your life. Can you think of a time when your mind was hassled with fears? Once you truly committed your problem to the Lord, did a supernatural peace flood your soul and relieve you from your anxieties? This is the first step that Paul urges you to take when worry, fear, and concerns are trying to take over your mind or emotions.

The second step Paul tells us to take is found in the word "supplication." The word "supplication" in Greek is the word *deisis*, which depicts a person who has some type of lack in his life and therefore pleads strongly for his lack to be met. The word *deisis* is translated several ways in the *King James Version*, including to beseech; to beg; or to earnestly appeal. This word pictures a person in such great need that he feels compelled to push his pride out of the way so he can boldly, earnestly, strongly, and passionately cry out for someone to help or assist him.

One of the most powerful examples of the word *deisis* is found in James 5:16. In this famous verse of Scripture, the Bible says, "...The effectual fervent prayer of a righteous man availeth much." Here the word *deisis* is translated as "fervent prayer." You see, *deisis* is a passionate, earnest, heartfelt, sincere prayer. It comes to God on the most serious terms, strongly beseeching Him to move and to meet a specific need that the person praying is facing in his life.

So when you are facing a problem that deeply concerns you, don't be afraid to go to the Lord and earnestly beseech Him to meet your need. Paul's use of this word means you can get very bold when you ask God to move on your behalf. There is no reason for you to be timid or mealy-mouthed when you pray. You can tell God exactly what you feel, what you're facing, and what you want Him to do for you. This is what "supplication" is all about!

After mentioning "supplication," Paul then gives us the third important step to take when giving our worries and concerns to the Lord. Paul tells us to make our requests known to God "...by prayer and supplication with thanksgiving...."

God not only expects you to be bold; He also expects you to thank Him for being good to you! It simply isn't right to ask boldly without expressing thanksgiving. If you've ever generously given to someone who never took the time to thank you for the sacrifice you made for him or her, you know how shocking ingratitude can be. In a similar way, you must be careful to thank God for being so good to you!

The word "thanksgiving" that Paul uses in this verse is the Greek word *eucharistia*, which is a compound of the words *eu* and *charis*. The word *eu* means good or well. It denotes a general good disposition or an overwhelmingly good feeling about something. The word *charis* is the Greek word for grace. When these two words are compounded into one, they form the word *eucharistia*. This compound word describes an outpouring of grace and of wonderful feelings that freely flow from the heart in response to someone or something.

By using this word, Paul teaches us that when we earnestly ask God to do something special for us, we must match it with an earnest outpouring of thanks. Although the request has only just been made and the manifestation isn't evident yet, it is appropriate to thank God for doing what we have requested. Thanking Him in advance demonstrates faith.

So always make sure to follow up your earnest asking with earnest thanksgiving! Make it a goal to be just as passionate in your thanksgiving as you were when you made your request.

Paul then gives you the fourth step out of worry and anxiety when he tells you, "...Let your requests be made known unto God." The word "requests" is the Greek word *aitima*, from the word *aiteo*. The Greek word "ask" destroys any religious suggestion that you are a lowly worm who has no right to come into the Presence of God. You see, the Greek word *aiteo* means to be adamant in requesting and demanding assistance to meet tangible needs, such as food, shelter, money, and so forth.

In fact, in the New Testament, the word *aiteo* is used to portray a person who insists or demands that a specific need be met after approaching and speaking to his superior with respect and honor. Additionally, it expresses the idea that one possesses a full expectation to receive what was firmly requested.

There is no doubt that this word describes someone who prays authoritatively, in a sense demanding something from God. This person knows what he needs and is so filled with faith that he isn't afraid to boldly come into God's Presence to ask and expect to receive what he has requested.

This means when you pray about a need that concerns you, it is right for you to pray authoritatively. As long as your prayer is based on the Word of God, you can have the assurance of God's promise regarding the issue you are most concerned about. Furthermore, when you pray, it is spiritually appropriate for you to fully expect God to honor His Word and do what you have requested.

As a final, fifth point, Paul says, "...let your requests be made known unto God." The word "known" comes from the word *gnoridzo*, and it means to make a thing known; to declare something; to broadcast something; or to make something very evident. This plainly means that your asking can be extremely bold! Declare to God what you need; broadcast it so loudly that all of Heaven hears you when you pray. You can be exceptionally bold when you come before Jesus to make your requests known!

An expanded, interpretive translation of Philippians 4:6 could be rendered:

"Don't worry about anything — and that means nothing at all! Instead, come before God and give Him the things that concern you so He can, in exchange, give you what you need or desire. Be bold to strongly, passionately, and fervently make your request known to God, making certain that an equal measure of thanksgiving goes along with your strong asking. You have every right to ask boldly, so go ahead and insist that God meet your need. When you pray, be so bold that there is no doubt your prayer was heard. Broadcast

it! Declare it! Pray boldly until you have the assurance that God has heard your request!"

So, in moments when worry or fear is trying to wrap its life-draining tentacles around you, rush to the truths found in Philippians 4:6. You don't have to live subject to worry, concerns, and fears the rest of your life. If you follow these steps, worry and fear will always be replaced with a peaceful and praising heart!

Why don't you take the time today to enter God's Presence and walk through these five important steps? It's time to move from fear to faith, from turmoil to peace, and from defeat to victory!

My Prayer for Today

Lord, I thank You for allowing me to come boldly before You in prayer. I know that You love me and want to richly meet the needs I am facing in my life today. My temptation is to worry and fear, but I know that if I will trust You, everything I am concerned about will turn out all right. Right now, I reject the temptation to worry, and I choose to come before You to boldly make my requests known. By faith, I thank You in advance for acting to answer my requests!

I pray this in Jesus' name!

My Confession for Today

I confess that I am not ruled by worry, fear, or concerns. I go to God with those things that are on my heart, and I clearly articulate what I feel, what I need, and what I expect Heaven to do on my behalf. Because of the promises in God's Word, I know exactly how to boldly make my requests. I always match my requests with thanksgiving, letting God know how grateful I am for everything He does in my life. Heaven is on my side, therefore, I know I will survive and victoriously overcome each and every attack that ever tries to come against my family, my relationships, my business, my finances, and my life.

I declare this by faith in Jesus' name!

Questions for You to Consider

1. When worry, fears, and concerns try to overwhelm you, what do you do in response? Do you give in and allow worry and fretfulness to fill your mind, or do you run to the Lord and commit your problems to Him?

   _____

   _____

   _____

   _____

   _____

   _____

2. Can you recall times in your life when you gave an all-consuming worry to the Lord? In return, did He fill you with supernatural peace, enabling you to overcome the worries that were trying to devour you?

   _____

   _____

   _____

   _____

   _____

3. What new truth did you learn from today's lesson? If these truths were helpful to you, can you think of someone else you know who needs this same encouragement? If so, why don't you contact that friend today to encourage him or her from the Word of God?

_____

_____

_____

_____

_____

_____

Day 8

Grace, Mercy, and Peace

> *Unto Timothy, my own son in the faith: Grace, mercy, and peace....*
>
> **— 1 Timothy 1:2**

I f you've ever felt like problems were mounting and growing all around you, and you didn't have enough strength to make it another step, then I have some very good news for you! Today you're going to discover that God extends a very special measure of mercy to people who feel like they are being swamped by the affairs of life. Stay with me, because what you're about to read is exactly what you need to start your day!

In all of the apostle Paul's epistles, he begins by greeting his readers with "grace" and "peace." The exact wording from letter to letter may vary, but each of these epistles begin with some variation of a greeting that involves the words "grace" and "peace." (*see* Romans 1:7; 1 Corinthians 1:3; 2 Corinthians 1:2;

Galatians 1:3; Ephesians 1:2; Philippians 1:2; Colossians 1:2; 1 Thessalonians 1:1; 2 Thessalonians 1:2; and Philemon 1:3).

Why did Paul so often use these two words in his greetings when he wrote his epistles? The answer is very simple. Because he was an apostle to the Gentiles or the Greek-speaking world, it was necessary for him to greet his foremost readers in a customary Greek manner. During New Testament times, the salutation of "grace" was the customary greeting exchanged between Greeks when they approached each other. Just as we would say, "Hello, how are you doing?" as a polite way of greeting someone we meet, the Greeks would say, "Grace!" when greeting one another.

This word "grace" is the Greek word *charis*, which means grace but also carries the idea of favor. So when a person greeted someone with this salutation, it was the equivalent of his saying, "I greet you with grace and favor."

But Paul wasn't only addressing the Greek world. As a Jew himself, he also wanted to greet the Jewish world that would be reading his epistles. When the Jews met each other, their customary way of greeting one another was to say, "Shalom!" In fact, this is still the customary greeting exchanged between Jews in Israel today. The Greek equivalent for the Hebrew word *shalom* is the word *eirene*, which is the word for peace.

By using both of these two greetings at the beginning of his epistles, Paul brilliantly reached out and embraced both the Greek and the Jewish world at the outset of his writings. One scholar has said that by using both the terms "grace" and "peace," the doors were thrown open for the whole world to read his letters. It is obvious that Paul deliberately addressed those letters to both the Gentile and Jewish world.

Because of the meaning of the words *charis* and *eirene* and how these words were used as a form of greeting, it is as though Paul was saying:

"To those of you who are Greeks, I greet you with grace and favor, and to those of you who are Jews, I greet you with peace and shalom."

When Paul wrote the books of First Timothy, Second Timothy, and Titus, he inserted the word "mercy" between the words "grace" and "peace" in his greeting, making the salutation read "grace, mercy, and peace from God our Father." In all three of these epistles, he was not writing to an entire congregation; rather, these letters were private letters intended to be read only by Timothy and Titus.

Why did Paul alter his traditional greeting to include the word "mercy" when he wrote these personal letters? Well, in all three of these letters, Paul was writing to someone in the ministry who felt overwhelmed by the affairs of life. For instance, when he wrote his first letter to Timothy (the book of First Timothy), Timothy was feeling overwhelmed by the phenomenal growth in the church under his care. Such growth is every pastor's dream; however, Timothy was young, and he was pastoring what had become the world's largest church. This was, therefore, a very challenging time in Timothy's life.

Timothy was feeling so challenged that he apparently wrote a letter to Paul, asking him for advice on how to choose leaders for his fast-growing congregation. As the young minister faced this daunting task, he needed to be reminded that there was special "mercy" available to help him in his time of need. Thus, when Paul wrote to Timothy, he inserted the word "mercy" between the traditional greeting of "grace" and "peace." He said, "Unto Timothy, my own son in the faith: Grace, mercy, and peace..." (1 Timothy 1:2).

Several years after Paul wrote that first letter to Timothy, the political environment in the Roman Empire radically changed and public opinion turned violently against believers. Just as the Church had grown quickly before this change occurred, it now began to quickly diminish as believers were captured, imprisoned, enslaved, and killed. Many believers also defected from the

Christian faith and went back to their old pagan temples in order to comply with the wishes of the government and to save themselves from death.

The tragedy occurring inside Timothy's church was devastating. The size of his prized congregation was declining daily right before his eyes. His heart was broken as he watched leaders defecting and going back to their old ways in order to escape death — trusted team members who Timothy had thought would be faithful to the very end.

Apparently, Timothy had written a letter to Paul, expressing his fears and hurts about the crisis he faced, so Paul wrote him back. That second letter to Timothy (the book of Second Timothy) is Paul's response to Timothy and to the predicament that surrounded the younger minister on every side. Writing Timothy to encourage him to be strong in the Lord, Paul began his second letter by once more inserting the word "mercy" between the words "grace" and peace." He said, "To Timothy, my dearly beloved son: Grace, mercy, and peace..." (2 Timothy 1:2).

The third time Paul inserted the word "mercy" between his traditional greetings of "grace" and "peace" was in his letter to Titus. As with Timothy, Titus found himself in a very difficult circumstance. After Paul started the church on the island of Crete, he left before the church was completely established and before leaders were firmly set in place. Paul left Titus to finish the job he didn't complete in Crete, instructing him to make the final selection of church leaders and then establish them in their positions.

The people who lived on Crete at that time were famous for being lazy, gluttons, and liars. They were a devious, mischievous people who were very difficult to trust. Even more, Crete was known to be a repository for criminals and barbaric-like people. Paul wrote to Titus and told him, "For this cause left I thee in Crete, that thou shouldest set in order the things that are wanting..." (Titus 1:5). This would have been a monstrous task for even the most seasoned leader, and it loomed before Titus as a huge and daunting assignment.

The circumstances Titus faced were so immense that when Paul wrote to him, he said, "To Titus, mine own son after the common faith: Grace, mercy, and peace..."(Titus 1:4). It wasn't enough for Titus to hear about grace and peace — he also needed to be reminded that there was special mercy available to help him in his situation.

In all three of these cases, the readers were facing serious situations and needed to be reminded that God's mercy was extended to help them bravely face and overcome their challenges.

You may need to be reminded of the same thing today. If you are facing a situation that would normally be devastating or overwhelming to you, grab hold of this good news: God has made a special measure of His "mercy" available to you! Don't try to face the ordeal in your own strength until you end up feeling swamped and overwhelmed; instead, realize that God's mercy is available to meet you right where you are. If you'll open your heart to receive from God, He will tuck a special measure of mercy between the grace and peace He is offering you today. So why don't you allow God's mercy to assist you with the challenges you are facing at this very moment?

My Prayer for Today

Lord, I thank You for making special mercy available to help me in times of struggle and hardship. I admit that I often try to handle all my challenges on my own, but I know it is impossible for me to overcome my obstacles without the help of Your mercy. So today, I am opening my heart and asking You to extend a special measure of mercy to assist me through this challenging time in my life. I thank You in advance for pouring this mercy upon me, and by faith, I receive it right now.

I pray this in Jesus' name!

My Confession for Today

I confess that God's mercy is working in me! God promises mercy to me, and I receive it by faith. That mercy empowers me to overcome my negative emotions, my struggles, and all the obstacles the devil has tried to set before me. Because God's mercy is working in me, I am well able to rise above the struggles I face and overcome them victoriously!

I declare this by faith in Jesus' name!

Questions for You to Consider

1. Can you think of a time when you were suddenly invigorated by a supernatural flow of divine mercy that surged into you and gave you the strength and courage you needed to face and overcome a difficult situation?

_____

_____

_____

_____

_____

_____

2. When you became aware of that special mercy, how did it affect both your attitude and the situation you were facing?

_____

_____

_____

_____

_____

_____

3. If you are especially challenged by a situation in your life right now, why not take a few minutes today to ask God to give you a special measure of mercy to help?

_____

_____

_____

_____

_____

_____

Day 9

Do Your Best to Be at Peace with Everyone

> *If it be possible, as much as lieth in you, live peaceably with all men.*
>
> — Romans 12:18

D o you know anyone who rubs you the wrong way so badly that when you walk away from that person you feel like you're about to explode? Does it seem like that person always says something so rude, unkind, impolite, or derogatory that it nearly makes your blood boil when you are with him or her? Well, consider this: Have you ever had the thought that you may be rubbing that person the wrong way as well?

As I relate the following story to you, I am obligated by God to begin by telling you that, over the course of many years, the enemy I am about to describe became a friend. In fact, he is so dear to me today that I cherish every time I get to see and spend time with him. So I testify to you from the onset that the majority of horrible relational situations can be turned around if you will obey what Romans 12:18 tells you to do. That is what I want to talk to you about today.

Many years ago, I had to regularly deal with a pastor who was one of the rudest and most belittling people I had ever met in my life. But the man lived in the same city as I did, so I couldn't avoid seeing him from time to time. Whenever he and I found ourselves in the same room, I was nearly always shocked at what came out of his mouth. He freely gossiped and spoke malicious things about other pastors and churches. Everyone was his target — including me!

Because he was a pastor in our same city, I tried very hard to get along with him. But he was one of those people who simply rubbed me the wrong way, and I just didn't like him. And I definitely didn't like being near him! I repeatedly asked the Lord to help me forgive the callous words he had spoken about me to other pastors and leaders. Because he and I were pastors of the two largest churches in that particular nation, I knew I had to get along with this man. Nevertheless, trying to draw close to him was like trying to hug a cactus. I got jabbed and stabbed every time I came close!

I tried to convince myself that my inner conflict with this pastor was the result of a wrong mix of personalities. But if that were the case, this man had a wrong personality mix with every pastor in our city! The truth was that he was simply an offensive person. He knew he was offensive; he enjoyed it; and he had no intention of changing. And the way he affected me was exactly the way every other pastor I knew felt as well.

After many years of struggling in my relationship with this man, I finally came to realize that although this man was mightily gifted as a public communicator, he had no people skills on a personal level. He really was ill-mannered. The problem truly was him. Because this pastor respected no one but himself and was not submitted to any spiritual authority, no one could find a way to speak into his life to help him.

So what was I to do in this situation? As I said, he and I were each pastors of the two largest churches in our city, so we were continually attending meetings in which both of us were expected to participate. Like it or not, I was going to regularly be in this man's company. It was impossible for me to avoid the man, so I began to ask the Lord to help me know how to get along with him, so I didn't leave upset every time the two of us had to be at the same place.

The Holy Spirit led me to Romans 12:18. It says, "If it be possible, as much as lieth in you, live peaceably with all men." This verse gave me direction. It provided helpful answers that enabled me to deal successfully with this difficult situation. And I believe these answers will also help you know how to deal with that person who constantly rubs you the wrong way!

Notice that the apostle Paul began this verse by saying, "If it be possible...." The fact that he began with the word "if" — the Greek word *ei*, which is like an open question mark with no definitive answer — means there may be times when we run into a case where it is not possible to have peace with all men. As we are probably all well aware, it can be very difficult to be at peace with some people — not necessarily because we are so difficult, but because they are hard to get along with. But remember, they may think the same of us! But regardless of the difficulty of the task or the ugly behavior of those we encounter along the way in life, the command of God remains: To the best of our ability, we must give our best efforts to be at peace with all men.

The word "possible" comes from the Greek word *dunaton*. In this verse, it expresses the idea of something that is potentially difficult but nonetheless doable. But because this phrase begins with the word "if," it casts a shadow on whether or not it is truly doable. Maybe peace is attainable; maybe it isn't. But if it is doable, you are to give it your best shot. For this reason, this phrase could be translated: "If it is doable..."; "If it is feasible..."; or as the *King James Version* translates it, "If it is possible...."

Paul continued to say, "...As much as lieth in you, live peaceably with all men." The words "as much as lieth in you" come from a mixture of Greek words that means "as far as it depends on you." This phrase points toward you and me, placing the responsibility of maintaining peace and a good attitude on us, not on the person we find to be so offensive. This clearly means that God is expecting us to do everything we can from our perspective and to give it our best to "live peaceably with all men."

The words "live peaceably" are from the word *eireneuo*, a form of the word *eirene*, which means to live in peace or to possess peace. In Romans 12:18, it carries this idea: "Once you've finally obtained peace, you must determine that you are going to do your best to make sure it is maintained and kept." In other words, instead of being a contributor to the problem, you are to do all you can to be a facilitator of peace!

And notice that Paul said we are to do this with "all men." In my case, these words "all men" meant I had to live peaceably with the ill-mannered pastor who continually upset me with his offensive behavior. But the words the Holy Spirit used in this verse are unquestionable. The words "all men" is a translation of the words *panton anthropon*. The word *panton* is an all-encompassing word that means everyone. The word *anthropon* comes from *anthropos*, the Greek word that describes all of mankind, including every male and female of every race, nationality, language, religion, and skin color — no one excluded. There is no phrase in Greek that could be more all-encompassing than *panton anthropon*. It literally embraces the entire human race. It does not say we have to agree with all people or condone their behavior — but as much as it depends on us, we are to be at peace with them. At the very moment Paul wrote this verse, he and other Christians were facing horrible pagan and religious opposition from those who had no tolerance for "narrow-minded" believers. Yet it was at this same time that the Holy Spirit commanded them through this verse to do everything they could to get along with everyone.

And this same divine command is directed toward us. It doesn't say to live peaceably only with friends, family, peers, or those who agree with us. It says that if it's possible, we are to live at peace "with all men." An interpretive version of Romans 12:18 could be rendered: "If it's doable at all, then as much as depends on you, be at peace with everyone, no one excluded."

This verse was so helpful to me when I was learning how to get along with that ill-mannered pastor. I understood that Jesus did not expect me to be his best friend, but Jesus did expect me to give it my best effort to live peacefully in that situation. If being at peace with him meant perhaps not engaging in a lengthy conversation with him, then whatever I had to do, I was determined not to live upset with this man who had been such a source of pain and irritation to me. I had to let it go, let God deal with him, and walk away from my hankering to fix or correct him. As much as it depended on me, from my side, I was going to do whatever was necessary to be at peace with him.

I know that you have relationships that trouble you, as this is true of everyone. If you're tired of getting upset, being irritated, or unsuccessfully trying to correct those individuals, perhaps you should choose the route of simply seeking to be at peace. Negotiation with a difficult person is not always possible, so sometimes the best option is simply doing whatever is necessary to be at peace. This was the message the Holy Spirit spoke to me, and I believe it is the message the Holy Spirit may be speaking to you right now as well.

So, if you're exhausted from trying to fix an unfixable relationship, and yet your contact with that person is inescapable, ask the Holy Spirit to help you deal with your own heart so that you can be at peace even with that person. That difficult relationship is part of the "all men" with whom the Holy Spirit commanded you to be at peace. As stated before, it doesn't mean that you have to agree with that person, condone what he or she does, or discard your beliefs to obtain peace. It simply means you choose not to enter into the fray with that person any longer. You'll be more at peace as a result, and you will be unmoved by the difficult people in your life because you have set yourself to be at peace with all men, regardless of what anyone says or does.

My Prayer for Today

Lord, I thank You for speaking to my heart today. I repent for my carnal response toward certain people in my life. I confess that I have allowed myself to become irritated with them, and at times I have even been judgmental of them. Today I release forgiveness toward them, and I choose from this point onward to see myself as a force for peace. I purpose in my heart to exercise the patience that is a quality of Your love within me. I ask You for wisdom to know what to say and do and what not to say and do when I am in the presence of these individuals. Thank You for leading and guiding me in each contact I make with them.

I pray this in Jesus' name!

My Confession for Today

I let the peace of God act as umpire continually in my heart, deciding and settling with finality all questions or concerns that arise in my mind. I refuse to be ruled by my emotions, and I am not moved by what I see, feel, or hear. I have the mind of Christ, and I hold the thoughts, feelings, and purposes of His heart. The wisdom of God determines my responses and reactions to those I consider ill-mannered or badly behaved who are not within my realm of authority to correct. I boldly declare that I will not live my life upset or bothered by something I cannot fix. Whatever is necessary to be at peace and to remain at peace is what I will do, as I have been commanded in Romans 12:18.

I declare this by faith in Jesus' name!

Questions for You to Consider

1. Have you ever considered that you may affect someone who rubs you the wrong way the same way that he or she affects you? Are you sure that you are not somehow contributing to the atmosphere you experience when you are with that person?

---

2. What do you need to do to eliminate the conflict between you and that individual? Since Romans 12:18 commands you to do everything from your side to be at peace, what steps do you need to take to obey that verse? Wouldn't it be worth your time to think this through and perhaps write down a few thoughts about what you could change or do differently to have peace with that individual?

---

3. Is it possible that the person who irritates you is ignorant of his insensitivity or has just never awakened to the impact he is having on others? Why don't you take a prayerful position for him and leave him in the hands of Jesus?

_____

_____

_____

_____

_____

Day 10

It's Time for You to Stop Wrestling and Start Resting!

> *There remaineth therefore a rest to the people of God. For he that is entered into his rest, he also hath ceased from his own works, as God did from his.*
>
> **— Hebrews 4:9,10**

When I was a young boy, I was terrified that I wasn't really saved. A powerful revivalist visited our church and preached a message that became etched into my mind about people who thought they were saved but weren't — people who died thinking they were going to Heaven but whose final destination was hell. That sermon terrified me!

Every night I went to bed troubled, thinking that if I died during the night, I would end up in hell. I had asked Jesus into my heart when I was five years old and had understood what I was doing. But after hearing that man's bloodcurdling sermon, I was gripped with fear that I might be among those who thought they were saved but were in fact lost.

Every night my mother would lie by my side and listen as I told her how frightened I was that I wasn't saved. She would hold me — her little six-year-old boy — and pray with me until I fell asleep each night.

That dread lingered in my life for many years. I can't count the times I prayed: "Dear Lord Jesus, I know I've asked You into my heart so many times before, but just in case I didn't really mean it all those other times, I am asking You to come into my heart again right now." I must have prayed that prayer 10,000 times.

Each time I felt a sigh of relief for a couple of hours — and then the panicky thought would hit me again: Maybe YOU are among those who just think they are saved but have never really been sincere! Maybe you are one of those who think they're going to Heaven but are going to end up in hell! This fear overwhelmed me. I found myself obsessed with the need to be saved, yet incapable of feeling secure that I was saved.

I silently cried out for inner peace as I dedicated and rededicated my life to the Lord. Over and over again at church, I'd lay before the altar and plead with God for peace of mind. Privately — at home, on the street, wherever I was — I'd beg God to reach down and rescue me. Every Sunday, when the pastor gave the invitation at the end of the service, he would ask the congregation to search their hearts to see if they were genuinely saved. Each week that question initiated the whole painful process all over again for me. I was living in torment.

If I called home as a teenager and no one answered the telephone, my heart would sink with the thought that the Rapture had occurred, and I had been left behind. I'd begin frantically calling members of our church, hoping someone would pick up the telephone. If a church member answered, it meant I had not been left behind!

When I was 24 and newly married, I was still intermittently struggling with this issue about my salvation. One day I fell on my knees at the altar of the large Baptist church where I worked as an associate pastor and cried out to the Lord: "This is it! I've spent most of my life trying to get saved. I've prayed 10,000 times for you to save me, and I'm finished asking! If I'm not saved, there is nothing more I can do to be saved, so I'm not asking again!"

The moment I prayed that prayer, the monstrous fear that had engulfed me for so many years of my life simply evaporated. For the first time in my life, I had the assurance that I was saved. The truth is, I'd been saved many years earlier at the age of five. But because a seed of fear had been sown into my heart by the preaching of that revivalist so many years earlier, I had never been able to "rest" in my salvation.

But on that day at that altar, I gave up my struggle of trying to be saved, and I made the decision to simply rest in God's grace. I realized that if His grace wasn't enough to do the work, all my asking and begging weren't going to make a difference anyway. At that moment, I quit wrestling and started resting. And that was the moment I finally began to enjoy my salvation!

When I read Hebrews 4:9 and 10, I always think of the rest that came to my soul when I finally accepted the fact that I was saved by grace. Oh, what a blessed day that was! I finally gave up my fight and accepted the salvation I had already received many years earlier as a young child. For so many years I'd been driven by fear — constantly asking, pleading, and begging, trying to prove my sincerity to the Lord. But all it took for me to be saved was to turn my heart to Jesus and receive Him as my Savior — and that's what I had done as a young child. I had been saved all along, but I had never learned to "rest" in my salvation.

Hebrews 4:9 says, "There remaineth therefore a rest to the people of God." Today I want us to look at several words in this verse. Let's begin with the word "rest."

The word "rest" in this verse comes from the Greek word *sabbatismos*, which is used in the Greek Septuagint version of the Old Testament to refer to the Sabbath day. This means Hebrews 4:9 should really be translated, "There remaineth therefore a Sabbath rest to the people of God."

What does "Sabbath rest" mean in the context of this verse? Let's go back to the book of Genesis just for a moment. God worked for six days when He created the heavens and earth. At the end of those six days, the Bible tells us that when God looked at everything He had made, it was so perfect, complete, finished, and flawless, He knew there was nothing else that could be added to it. It was a complete, finished work that required nothing more. Since this masterpiece of creation was completely finished, the biblical record tells us that God "rested" from his labor on the seventh day and simply enjoyed creation.

In Genesis 2:2 and 3, we read, "And on the seventh day God ended his work which he had made; and he rested on the seventh day from all his work which he had made. And God blessed the seventh day, and sanctified it: because that in it he had rested from all his work which God created and made."

This day when God "rested" was the first official Sabbath day — the day when God rested from all His work. Later, when Moses received the Ten Commandments, God explicitly ordered the children of Israel to remember the Sabbath day and to keep it holy. So every week on the Sabbath day, the children of Israel ceased from all labor and rested as a way of honoring the day when God rested from His own works. Therefore, the Sabbath was a day of unbroken rest and cessation from work.

By telling us, "There remaineth therefore a Sabbath rest to the people of God," the Bible declares that the people of God can rest in their salvation once they have given their lives to Jesus Christ. His work on the Cross was so complete, perfect, finished, and flawless that there is nothing anyone can do to add to it. A person isn't brought any closer to salvation by asking, begging, pleading, and imploring God to be saved or by trying to prove his sincerity so he can be worthy of salvation. If a person has given his life to Christ, he can "rest" in the fact that it is a done deal. Instead of struggling the way I did as a young man, every person who has trusted in Christ can relax, unwind, calm down, lighten up, and rest in the completed work of God that was purchased on the Cross of Jesus Christ!

Just as I did years ago, you must also make a decision to give up your struggle of trying to be saved and make the decision to simply rest in God's grace. If God's grace isn't enough to do the job, all of your asking and begging isn't going to make a difference anyway. It's time for you to quit wrestling and start resting so you can begin to enjoy your salvation!

Hebrews 4:10 continues to tell us, "For he that is entered into his rest, he also hath ceased from his own works, as God did from his."

The word "entered" is the Greek word *eiserchomai*. It is a compound of the words *eis* and *erchomai*. The first part of the word means into. The second part of the word *erchomai* means to go. It gives the idea of a person who is traveling or journeying to some destination. When these words are compounded into one, as they are in this verse, it forms the word *eiserchomai*, which expresses the idea of a person who enters into a certain place. He doesn't just come near to this location; he actually enters into that location.

This means that those who have given their lives to Jesus Christ have entered into the completed work of God that occurred on the Cross of Jesus Christ.

Yes, the moment Jesus became Lord of your life was the exact split second you entered into God's completed work of salvation. Regardless of what the devil may try to whisper to make you think that you must do more to really be saved, the fact remains that if your life has been given to Jesus Christ, you have already entered into the perfect, complete, finished, and flawless work of God. There is nothing you can add to it, so instead of allowing tormenting fear to steal your joy, it's time for you to quit struggling and start resting in what Jesus has done for you. You can calm down, relax, and be at peace!

The rest of the verse says, "For he that is entered into his rest, he also hath ceased from his own works, as God did from his." This verse says it's time for you to rest in this perfect, complete, finished, flawless work, just as God did on the seventh day when He was assured that His work of creation was done.

If you are resting in Christ's work, then you can rest from your work! That's why this verse continues to say, "For he that is entered into his rest, he also hath ceased from his own works, as God did from his." This word "cease" is the word *katapauo* — a compound of the words *kata* and *pauo*. The word *kata* means down, and the word *pauo* means to pause. When these words are compounded, the new word gives the idea of someone who has worked hard, but now has sat down, settled down, and has ceased from his labor. This is the picture of a person who has thrown off his work clothes and is now reclining in a restful position! You might say that he has finished his work and entered into retirement! The work is behind him, and that phase of his life is done and over. He is entering into a lasting and permanent rest.

So I want to encourage you today: If you struggle with your salvation, wondering whether or not you are really saved, nail it down forever by praying one last prayer of repentance and surrendering your life to Jesus Christ. Then walk away from that place of commitment and never revisit it again. Instead of habitually asking over and over to be saved, just pray in faith that God's Word is true, quit struggling, and start resting in what Jesus has done for you!

There is a "Sabbath rest" for the people of God, and it belongs to every person who simply comes in faith to Jesus Christ. If you belong to Him, it is high time for you to kick back and rest in the fact that Jesus saved you and that this work of redemption is utterly complete. Just make the decision today that from this day forward, you are going to enjoy the benefits of this wonderful salvation that Jesus purchased for you on the Cross!

My Prayer for Today

Lord, I thank You that You died on the Cross for me and purchased my salvation. Thank You for saving me from sin and its penalty. Thank You that there is nothing I can do to add to Your work on the Cross. Today I am making the decision to quit struggling about my salvation and to simply rest in the salvation You have provided for me. I asked You to save me, and You saved me. I asked You to forgive me, and You forgave me. From this day forward, I will rest in the complete work of redemption that You purchased for me with Your precious blood. Thank You, Jesus, for saving me!

I pray this in Jesus' name!

My Confession for Today

I confess that I am saved, forgiven, and born again by the Spirit of God. I asked Jesus to save me, and He saved me. I asked Jesus to forgive me, and He forgave me. I asked Jesus to come into my life, and now He lives in me by His Spirit. In Him I have redemption, deliverance, and salvation through His blood. In Christ I have the complete removal and forgiveness of sin in accordance with the generosity of God's great goodness and favor toward me (see Ephesians 1:7). I am as saved as a person can be! I refuse to let the devil torment me, steal my joy, or make me think that I haven't done enough to be saved. There is nothing I can add to the work of the Cross, so I am simply going to rest in what Jesus has already done for me!

I declare this by faith in Jesus' name!

Questions for You to Consider

1. What was the actual time in your life when you repented, asked Jesus Christ into your heart, and gave Him control of your life? Can you actually refer to the moment this happened?

   _____

   _____

   _____

   _____

   _____

   _____

2. Have you ever struggled with your salvation and wondered if you were really saved? How did you end this personal struggle and find peace of mind?

   _____

   _____

   _____

   _____

   _____

   _____

3. What would you say to someone else who is struggling with the question of whether or not he is really saved? What advice would you give that person, and what would you tell him or her to do to permanently find peace of mind?

_____

_____

_____

_____

_____

_____

Day 11

What to Do When Your Spirit Is Inwardly Disturbed

> *I had no rest in my spirit, because I found not Titus my brother: but taking my leave of them, I went from thence into Macedonia.*
>
> — 2 Corinthians 2:13

Many years ago, I developed an uneasy feeling about a longtime member of our team who worked in a leadership position in our ministry. However, because this person had always been faithful during his years with our organization, I tried to shrug off this uneasiness and ignore what I was feeling. Naturally speaking, there was no reason for me to be suspicious of him or to question his activities. All outward signs said he was doing an excellent job, yet I kept getting a gnawing feeling in my spirit that I should no longer trust him. To put it simply, I was deeply troubled on the inside and knew something was wrong.

When an occasion would arise for this man and me to be together, I'd look deeply into his eyes when he spoke to see if I could detect whether there was something he was trying to hide. When he spoke, I'd listen carefully to his words to see if there was anything misleading in what he told me. I took notice of his gestures, trying to ascertain whether or not he was acting nervous in my presence because he had something to hide. From all outward signs, everything seemed normal — yet inwardly, I was still extremely disturbed.

I would tell Denise, "I don't know what it is, but I sense that something is wrong with that person. Is God speaking to my spirit, or am I just being suspicious and untrusting of someone who has been faithful for a long time?" Because I could never put my finger on anything this man had done wrong, I decided that I was the problem — that I was being overly suspicious and needed to stop being so skeptical and wary of this devoted employee.

For the next year, I tried hard to shake off those uneasy feelings, but I just couldn't do it. Even though I couldn't identify a specific problem, I inwardly knew that things on the surface were not as they really seemed concerning this employee.

After a year of struggling with this issue, I discovered that this man had been acting fraudulently on many fronts. It wasn't just a case of someone doing something wrong by accident; this was purposeful wrongdoing and manipulation of the truth for his own advantage. He had been conniving and deliberately misleading. I was shocked when I discovered the length and breadth he had gone to deceive me and our other leaders.

By the time I made my discovery of what this employee had been doing, severe damage had already been done in that department of our organization.

But the truth is, the Holy Spirit had been warning me of the problem for a very long time. That inward uneasiness I had experienced was His warning to me to back away from this man!

God's Spirit was trying to save me from the troubles produced by this employee who was conspiring against the work of the Gospel. If I had listened to my heart and followed what I sensed on the inside, I could have avoided the pain this man tried to bring about in our lives. I praise God that when I finally made this discovery, I had the courage to take fast action and terminate this attack!

From this experience that took place so many years ago, I learned the important lesson of paying attention when my spirit is inwardly disturbed. Very often this is God's way of giving us an alert signal that something is not right or that something is not as it seems on the surface.

That's why you must learn to pay attention when your spirit is inwardly troubled. Set aside some time to spend with the Lord, and ask the Holy Spirit to help you quiet your mind and emotions so He can reveal to you anything you need to know about the situation. Back up and take a good look at what is happening around you, and be willing to see the truth — even if it is something you'd rather not acknowledge! If you find that everything is fine, you can then move forward with the confidence that you did your homework. But if you find out that something is wrong, you'll be thankful you listened to your spirit and slowed down so you could make this discovery in order to deal with it — for your sake and the sake of others who may be adversely affected by it!

So ask yourself these questions:

🌿 Have you ever had an inward uneasiness or a lack of peace that you later wished you hadn't ignored?

🔥 Can you think of a time when the Holy Spirit tried to warn you of a problem, but you didn't listen to your heart and therefore ended up with a problem that could have been avoided?

🔥 Have you discovered that God is often speaking to you when you have a lack of peace in your heart — and that He is trying to tell you to back up and slow down, and to take a more cautious approach to what you are doing?

This kind of inward disturbance must be what Paul experienced when he came to the city of Troas and didn't find Titus waiting for him there. Although this exact event isn't recorded in the book of Acts, Paul mentioned it in his second letter to the Corinthian church. On one of his missionary journeys, Paul came to Troas, expecting to find Titus waiting for him. Paul was so taken aback that Titus wasn't there that he wrote, "I had no rest in my spirit, because I found not Titus my brother: but taking my leave of them, I went from thence into Macedonia" (2 Corinthians 2:13).

The word "rest" that Paul used in this verse comes from the Greek word *anesis*, which means to let up, to relax, to stop being stressed, or to find relief. In the Greek world, this word *anesis* could denote the release of a bowstring that had been under great pressure. Hence, it suggests the idea of relief. When used on a personal level, the word *anesis* depicts a person who has been under some type of pressure for a long time but has suddenly found a release from that pressure. You could say that this person has decided he is going to shake off and let go of whatever has been bothering him or the pressure he has been under.

However, Paul told us he could not shake off what he was inwardly feeling in his spirit. He was so restless or inwardly disturbed that he immediately left Troas and went on to Macedonia to search for his dear friend Titus. The phrase "taking my leave of them" is very strong in the Greek. It lets us know that Paul didn't take a long time to respond to this inward disturbance in his spirit; rather, he took it as a God-given signal that something wasn't right. Hence, Paul bade the believers in Troas farewell and quickly traveled to Macedonia to seek out his missing ministry friend.

Unlike my own scenario that I just related to you, the apostle Paul listened to his spirit. He knew that if he was inwardly disturbed, it could be a warning sign that something was wrong. Thus, he responded with urgency and took appropriate action when he had this kind of inner witness. How I wish I had done the same thing years ago! If I had listened to what my spirit was telling me, I could have avoided the many troubles that leader tried to create for me and for our ministry.

In light of all this, Second Corinthians 2:13 could be paraphrased:

> *"Regardless of how hard I tried to shake off a sense of inward disturbance, in my spirit I knew something was wrong. I tried to shake it off and let it go, but inwardly, I knew things were not right."*

As believers, we must learn to pay attention to the lack of peace we feel in our spirits. Sometimes that lack of peace or inward disturbance is God's way of alerting us to something important or of telling us that something isn't right. God lovingly tries to spare us from problems and catastrophes. However, if we don't pay attention to the still, small voice in our hearts when the Holy Spirit tenderly speaks to us, we will end up with troubles that could have been altogether avoided or corrected before they got out of hand.

God is faithful to speak to you — but His voice can often be heard only by what you sense in your own heart. If you sense peace in your heart, it could be the Holy Spirit telling you, "You have a green light, so you can proceed." But if you have a lack of peace or an inward disturbance, never forget that it could be God's way of saying, "Yellow light, so proceed with caution." Or He may even be telling you, "Red alert! Stop! Something is wrong!"

Don't make the mistake I made many years ago by ignoring that lack of peace in your heart. It will be far better for you if you take a little time to back up, slow down, and find out why you're feeling uneasy on the inside. If you find that everything is all right, you will then be able to move forward with assurance. But if you learn that something is not right, you'll be so thankful that you listened to your heart and got things in order before you proceeded any further and damage was done!

My Prayer for Today

Father, I thank You for Your Spirit, who is so faithful to alert me when things are not right. Please forgive me for the many times You tried to warn and help me, but I ignored Your voice and found myself in a mess I could have avoided. From this day forward, I am asking You to help me become more sensitive to my spirit. Help me pay attention to the peace or the lack of peace I inwardly sense so I can respond appropriately when You are trying to warn me that something isn't the way it should be.

I pray this in Jesus' name!

My Confession for Today

I confess that I am sensitive to the Spirit of God. When He speaks to my heart, I quickly respond to Him and obey His instructions. I hear His voice indicating when I have God's green light to move ahead; therefore, I step out in faith. When I sense God's yellow light to move slowly and with caution, I am careful and cautious. When my spirit is inwardly disturbed and I have no peace, I know that this is God's red light — one of the ways He alerts me that something is not right. Because I am sensitive to what God is telling me in my spirit, I am able to move forward with confidence that I am not going to make a mistake!

I declare this by faith in Jesus' name!

Questions for You to Consider

1. Can you think of a time when you were inwardly disturbed, but you ignored it — and then later found out it was God trying to warn you about something? When was that, and what happened?

_____

_____

_____

_____

_____

2. What did you learn from that experience when you ignored what you sensed in your spirit?

_____

_____

_____

_____

_____

3. When you sense an inward disturbance, a lack of peace, or a restlessness in your spirit, how should you respond to it?

_____

_____

_____

_____

_____

_____

Day 12

Follow After Peace

> *Follow peace with all men, and holiness, without which no man shall see the Lord....*
>
> **— Hebrews 12:14**

D o you have a difficult relationship in your life that has been poisoned by offense, bitterness, or misunderstanding? It doesn't matter who it is — your spouse, a sibling, a friend, an employee, or a member of your church — you will find vital keys to help you navigate the situation in Hebrews 12:14. The verse starts out by saying, "Follow peace with all men...."

That word "follow" is the Greek word *dioko*. This word was an old hunting term that meant to follow the tracks of the animal or to follow the scent of the animal. Just imagine a hunter decked out in all his hunting gear, and he's following the tracks of his prey. He's following the scent of the beast, and he's looking for every little branch that the animal may have broken. The hunter is hunting, following, and searching for that animal — and he is not going to stop until finally he gets his prey.

This word *dioko* is also translated as "persecute" in the New Testament. In other words, when someone was persecuted, it wasn't something done haphazardly or accidentally; persecution was very intentional and deliberate. The persecutor followed his intended victims. He searched for them. He hunted them. He tracked them down. He was out to get them.

Now the Holy Spirit uses this same word in Hebrews 12:14 and says, "Follow after peace with all men...." That means sometimes peace doesn't just come to us. In fact, most of the time, peace does not come to us. We have to do something to find peace with people. We have to follow after peace.

No matter how difficult a particular relationship in your life is, God is telling you in this verse what your responsibility is as a believer. You have to put on your hunting gear and make a firm decision to do something about that relationship according to His love that has been shed abroad in your heart (*see* Romans 5:5). Remind yourself: "I can't be responsible for what that person does, but I am responsible for what I do — and God has required me to do everything I can do to obtain peace in this relationship." Of course, sometimes when you do everything you can do, the other person doesn't respond. You can't answer for the other person, but you are going to answer for yourself.

So, if you're struggling to have peace with someone in your life, take this verse to heart. It's time to put on your hunting gear and begin to look for anything you can do. Follow the tracks. Follow the scent. Look for every little broken branch. Look for anything you might possibly do that might lead to peace. Follow the tracks of peace.

Why is it so important that we follow after peace? The Bible goes on to tell us the reason in Hebrews 12:14: "Follow peace with all men and holiness without which no man will see the Lord." That word "see" tells us that lack of peace serves as a blocker that stops us from being admitted into the immediate presence of God. Think how many times you've been in a service where God's anointing is present and people are being blessed, but you can't enter into it because you are so inwardly upset about someone or something. You see, these attitudes are blockers, and that is why the writer of Hebrews says without peace — or in the presence of strife — you will not be able to be admitted into the life-changing presence of God. Strife is a blocker. It will stop you from entering into the anointing. It will stop you from entering into blessing of any kind.

The Bible tells us to "follow after peace and holiness." The word "holiness" is the word *hagias*. It means to be separate or to be different. In this particular case, the writer of Hebrews is telling us that we don't have the privilege of acting or thinking like the world. God calls us to a higher standard. The Holy Spirit lives in us, giving us the power we need to walk in forgiveness on a much higher level than the world. The Holy Spirit gives us the power to walk in freedom rather than the bondage the world walks in. We are called to follow after peace — to hunt it, seek it, pursue it — with all men. And we're called to walk in holiness, to behave differently than lost people behave, and to walk in forgiveness, free from offense. If we fail to pursue that kind of spiritual walk and remain in strife and bitterness, we'll never really be able to experience the tangible presence of God.

Take a moment to look at your life. Think about those times when you've harbored bitterness and offense and allowed your heart to grow hard toward a person. It was very difficult for you to experience the sweet presence of the Lord during those times, wasn't it? That's what this verse is talking about.

God has called us to a higher level, and like it or not, this verse tells us what we have to do when we're dealing with difficult people in our lives who have hurt or offended us. If we're serious about being disciples of Jesus, we must determine to forgive every person and every offense. We have to respond differently than the world would respond. Then as much as is possible with us, we must actively follow after obtaining peace with every person.

And let me tell you, friend — the only way you're going to be able to do this is by spending time with Jesus. Ask Him what path you're to follow to obtain peace. No one understands this better than Jesus. He had enemies all around Him, yet He walked in peace with all men. Talk to Jesus, and He'll get you on the right track that leads to freedom from strife and offense and to an abiding sense of His presence every day of your life.

My Prayer for Today

Heavenly Father, Your Word is very clear on how I am to respond to people who have hurt or offended me. When I am dealing with difficulties in relationships, You expect me to take the responsibility of hunting down peace and pursuing it. I ask You to show me what path I am to take in this pursuit so that I can please You by walking in the high level of love You have already shed abroad in my heart by the Holy Spirit who was given to me. I will not allow hurt, bitterness, or resentment to separate me from Your immediate presence. I receive Your help, Holy Spirit, to maintain a pure heart so that not only can I see God, but also so that I can see others as He sees them.

I pray this in Jesus' name!

My Confession for Today

I confess that because the Holy Spirit lives in me, I have the power I need to walk in forgiveness on a much higher level than the world. The Holy Spirit gives me the power to walk in freedom from the bondage of bitterness and strife. God requires me to follow after peace — to hunt it, seek it, and pursue it — with all men. Therefore, because I am required to do it, I am equipped to do it. I yield to the Holy Spirit, and I walk in holiness and in consecration to God and His ways. I deliberately separate myself from ungodly attitudes and actions because I refuse to be separated from the presence of God.

I declare this by faith in Jesus' name!

Questions for You to Consider

1. Has there been a relationship in your life in which you have found it particularly difficult to maintain peace? Who is that other person? Do you know why it has been so difficult to keep that relationship peaceful? Do you remember how the whole mess began, and do you know what you would have done differently if you could start all over again?

_____

_____

_____

_____

_____

_____

_____

_____

_____

_____

_____

_____

_____

_____

_____

_____

2. Has the Holy Spirit told you to follow after peace with that person? Instead of waiting for him or her to come to you with an apology, why don't you put on your "hunting gear" and make the choice to start following after peace until you finally obtain it in that relationship? It may require some creative thinking and acting born of diligent prayer about the matter — but if the Holy Spirit tells you to do it, it means you can do it. Go for it!

_____

_____

_____

_____

_____

_____

_____

_____

_____

_____

_____

_____

_____

_____

_____

_____

_____

3. Have you been getting signals from the Holy Spirit that you have unresolved issues of hurt or offense with another person? For instance, when you try to worship God, does a certain name keep coming up, causing unsettled thoughts that steal your joy and your ability to freely worship? Don't ignore those kinds of signs. That may be the Holy Spirit telling you that strife is at work in your life to keep you from enjoying the presence of the Lord. If it's always the same person over and over again, consider that a clear signal that there is some kind of issue between you and that person and that you should do everything you can to forgive that person and to seek his or her forgiveness and make that relationship right so you can freely enjoy the sweet presence of the Lord again!

Day 13

Sitting in Front of 40 Sunlamps for 8 Hours!

> *Be careful for nothing: but in every thing by prayer and supplication with thanksgiving let your requests be made known unto God. And the peace of God, which passeth all understanding, shall keep your hearts and minds through Christ Jesus.*
>
> **— Philippians 4:6,7**

When our TV ministry first began in the former USSR, we needed low-hanging, directional lights for our studio. Our staff was inexperienced, but they were all we had, so I sent them out to search for lights we could use to illuminate the studio where we were going to be filming our TV programs. With great delight, they returned with 40 big lights that they were sure would work to light up the studio. For a week, the staff members carefully hung the lights in place and tested them. After being satisfied that the lights were exactly what we needed, they said, "OK, now we can begin to film new TV programs!"

I was excited that the studio was so well lit and that the low-hanging lights looked so professional. But our studio had no air-conditioning, which made the room very hot. To stay cool, I wore a dress shirt, tie, and suit jacket from the waist up — and from the waist down, I wore shorts and put each leg into a big bucket of cool water in an effort to cool down while we were filming. Even with my legs submerged in that water, sweat would pour from my brow, and I would have to wipe my forehead the whole time we filmed. However, on this particular day, it felt especially hot — much hotter than usual.

After two hours of non-stop filming under those 40 lights, I felt very hot, so I took my legs out of the buckets, untied my tie, unbuttoned my top shirt, and went outside to get some fresh air. When I walked into the edit suite where the producers were working, they were trying to adjust the colors on the camera, because my skin looked so red on the monitors. They twisted this knob and that knob, trying to get the color to look right. They were so focused on what they were looking at on the monitors that they never actually looked at me! Eventually I heard them say, "We think we've got it fixed. So, Rick, why don't you head back into the studio, and let's film more programs."

Once I resumed filming, I didn't stop again until I had filmed a total of eight hours of TV programs that day. It was a personal record for the most TV programs I had ever filmed in a single day.

But this time, when I walked out of the studio, the producers looked at me to congratulate me for completing such a successful day. When they saw me, they gasped. It was at that moment they realized the 40 lights they were so proud of — that I had been sitting in front of for eight hours — were sunlamps! My face was severely burned and red beyond imagination. Try to imagine what you would look like if you sat in front of 40 sunlamps for eight hours! To make matters worse, I had been sitting in shorts with my legs in two buckets of water, and the radiation from those lamps literally scorched my legs. But the worst of all was what happened to my eyes — I could hardly see because my eyes were so burned. And every time I blinked, it felt like shredded pieces of glass were being dragged across my eyes.

At that time, pharmaceutical products were scarce in the former Soviet Union, so there were no medications or ointments to put on my burnt body. Instead, a local doctor recommended that I be covered in sour cream and that I then be tightly wrapped in plastic, like Saran Wrap, to keep the moisture trapped around my body! So, I lay on the couch as Denise and her helpers literally doused me from head to toe in sour cream, and then had me roll over and over so the plastic would tightly stretch around me. My arms were trapped under the plastic; my legs were bound; I was immovable. I remember telling Denise that I felt like a huge enchilada!

Hour by hour, the pain increased all over my face and legs — every place that had been exposed to the 40 sunlamps. I cried because of the horrible pain in my eyes every time I blinked. We called a doctor in the United States who warned that it was possible I would wake up blind the next morning because I had spent eight straight hours looking directly into 40 sunlamps. Fear tried to grip my heart. Denise lovingly stayed right at my side the entire night to comfort me because of the pain that wracked my body. The pain in my eyes was especially horrific. Denise comforted me and reassured me that I would be able to see and that, by the grace of God, we were going to get through this horrific ordeal!

That night I shuddered with pain every time I blinked, and fear kept trying to sink its talons into my mind. So, to fight against that fear, I decided to meditate on Philippians 4:6,7. When the pain raged through my eyes, I would quote this verse and focus on the promise of God instead of my excruciating condition. I probably quietly spoke that passage to myself hundreds of times that night as I released all my faith that my eyes would be all right, regardless of the pain that tormented me throughout that seemingly endless night.

The first verse of this passage, Philippians 4:6, tells us not to worry about anything. It reads, "Be careful for nothing: but in everything by prayer and supplication with thanksgiving let your request be made known unto God." Honestly, it took all of my determination that night not to worry about my eyes.

But the verse commands us to present our supplications and requests to God with thanksgiving and to leave worry behind. So that night I cried out to God and made my request known, asking for my eyesight. Hour after hour, I expressed thanksgiving to the Lord and did my best to praise Him from a grateful, thankful heart in spite of the pain. Denise prayed with me and helped me keep giving thanks to God through the night.

I wish that I could tell you that night was my last experience with sour cream and plastic, but the doctor recommended that I continue this treatment over the course of a few more days. As I lay trapped in that plastic during those long days — smelling like sour cream and suffering from tremendous pain all over my eyes, face, hands, and legs — I especially focused on God's promise in Philippians 4:7. This verse specifically held me in peace during that difficult time, and it has done so again and again throughout the years as I've continued to walk with Jesus. Verse 7 says, "And the peace of God, which passeth all understanding, shall keep your hearts and minds through Christ Jesus."

The word "peace" is the Greek word *eirene* — a powerful, often-used word in the New Testament that describes tranquility experienced after the cessation of war. It conveys the idea that the conflict is over; the war is finished; victory is achieved; and it is time for tranquility and rest. I had already expressed my supplications and thanksgiving to God, so it was time for me to rest in the fact that the battle for my sight was won. Since I had fulfilled the conditions of verse 7, I rested and allowed tranquility to come over me, and that tranquility ministered "peace" to my soul when I desperately needed it.

As I experienced this peace of God, it spoke to me far louder than the pain. Inwardly I knew that the battle for my eyes was over and that they were going to be all right. And just as verse 7 promises, "the peace that passeth understanding" began to "keep" my heart and mind.

The word "passeth" is a form of the word *huperecho*, which denotes something that is superior or surpassing. Because nothing compares to it, it is in a category of its very own. Furthermore, because this Greek word is a participle, we know that the peace of God expresses itself in us continuously. Thus, when I claimed peace in my situation, it began to continuously work in my heart and soul.

The word "understanding" is a translation of the Greek phrase *panta noun*, which literally means all understanding. It encompasses everything connected to the mind or reason. God's peace surpasses all reasoning, all understanding, and all thoughts that enter and work through the mind. This means that even though my mind screamed in pain, God's peace surpassed its vehement voice and enabled me to hear His healing words.

Paul concludes verse 7 by saying, "...The peace of God, which passeth all understanding, shall keep your hearts and minds through Christ Jesus." The word "keep" is the Greek word *phroureo*, which means to guard. However, it specifically referred to soldiers whose mission was to stand guard at the gate of a city to decide who was permitted inside. They had the power to decide who entered and who was restricted from entering the city. The word "heart" is *kardia*, which describes the center of a person from which thoughts and affections flow, and "mind" is *noema*, the Greek word for thoughts.

When you take this entire picture conveyed in verse 7 into consideration, we see that the peace of God stands like a guard at the entrance to our hearts, affections, and thoughts. If we allow peace to work, it will say "yes" to healthy, positive thoughts that want to enter those "gates" to our lives. But if something negative, detrimental, or destructive wants to enter our hearts, affections, and thoughts, the peace of God acts as a guard to block it from gaining access inside us. Thus, the peace of God acts as a sentinel of our hearts and minds.

As I recovered from my 8-hour encounter with 40 sunlamps, scary, fear-filled thoughts tried to enter my heart and mind. But when I claimed Philippians 4:6 and 7, the peace of God stood at the door to my heart and mind and refused to allow negativity and fear to enter my heart. The peace of God — the guard to my heart and mind — threw open the gates for a positive, healing influence. As a result, I recovered completely.

If you find yourself in a difficult position, and fearful thoughts try to enter your mind and emotions to create havoc, be quick to apply Philippians 4:6,7 to your situation. Very simply, do the three requirements laid out in verse 6:

1. Refuse to worry.

2. Let your requests be made known unto God by prayer and supplication.

3. Express thanksgiving — because heartfelt thankfulness is a powerful force to lift you up!

4. As you fulfill these conditions, God will go to work to perform His promise in verse 7.

5. The peace of God will go to work for you, producing supernatural tranquility and rest for your soul.

6. That peace will surpass any other thoughts that are trying to make you fearful.

7. That peace will act as a guard to prevent wrong thoughts from entering your heart, mind, and emotions — and it will throw open the door for positive, faith-filled thoughts to find entrance to your mind as well!

Philippians 4:6,7 is a very powerful passage of Scripture. If you'll fulfill the conditions of verse 6, God will be faithful to fulfill His promise to you in verse 7. So, if you need a measure of peace in your life, you can assuredly know that God is anxiously waiting to fulfill His promises to you and to all those whose lives you touch. Just allow the grace of God to touch you today, and watch how He strengthens you as you shake off the chains of anxious, negative thinking!

My Prayer for Today

Father, I thank You for Philippians 4:6,7. Starting today, I ask You to help me fulfill the conditions in verse 6. And as I do, I expect You by faith to start performing the promise in verse 7 on my behalf. I thank You that Your peace will bring tranquility and rest to my soul and serve as a sentinel to prohibit detrimental, damaging, and negative thoughts from entering my heart. Jesus fought the battle for me; the war is won; and now it's time for peace to express its full power in me!

I pray this in Jesus' name!

My Confession for Today

I boldly confess that I refuse to worry as I let my requests be made known unto God. I give God thanks for working in my life. As a result, I will experience the peace of God, and it will work for me to produce supernatural tranquility and rest for my soul. That peace will surpass any thoughts that are trying to make me fearful. That peace will act as a guard to keep wrong thoughts from entering my heart — and it will throw open the door for positive, faith-filled thoughts to find entrance instead.

I declare this by faith in Jesus' name!

Questions for You to Consider

1. Can you remember a moment in your life when fearful thoughts assailed your heart and mind, but after prayer, the peace of God brought tranquility and rest to your soul?

   _____

   _____

   _____

   _____

   _____

   _____

2. Do you know any individuals who are struggling and need the encouragement found in this lesson? If you really care about them, why not share it with them and let it strengthen them for the fight they are in?

   _____

   _____

   _____

   _____

   _____

   _____

3. Does peace or anxiety rule you? If you tend to be tossed about by anxiety, I want to tell you emphatically that the peace of God is the best medication for the soul. Ask God today to let His peace that passes understanding go to work in your heart, mind, and emotions!

_____

_____

_____

_____

_____

_____

Day 14

Cast All Your Care on the Lord!

Casting all your care upon him; for he careth for you.

— 1 Peter 5:7

When we were constructing a huge church facility many years ago in the Republic of Latvia — a former Soviet nation where our family once lived and worked — worry and anxiety tried so hard to control me. In fact, worry nearly broke me until I really came to understand and embrace the meaning of First Peter 5:7.

At the time, no credit was available for building churches in that nation. This meant we had to believe for all the finances to come in quickly so we could pay cash as we constructed the massive facility. Then the local authorities gave us a deadline by which the building had to be complete and occupied; otherwise, there was a possibility we could lose everything we had invested. With this kind of pressure on me, I found myself continually worrying that we wouldn't have enough money to finish the project on time. I was constantly fighting thoughts about losing the building if we didn't make the deadline that the government had given us.

I would lie in bed at night, rolling this way and that way, turning again and again, unable to sleep because my stomach was churning with acid and my mind was spinning with doubts, worries, fears, reservations, and concerns. My heart pounded harder and harder each day and night as anxiety reached out its demonic fingers to grab hold of my emotions and twist them into a mangled mess of panic. My wife would tell me to quit worrying and start trusting the Lord, but instead of appreciating her advice, I only got angry that she wasn't worrying with me!

Finally one night, I got up, walked down the hallway to my study, opened my Bible, and read these words: "Casting all your care upon him; for he careth for you" (1 Peter 5:7). I had read this verse thousands of times in my life, but that night it was as if it reached out from the pages of the Bible and grabbed hold of my attention. I read it and read it and read it again. At last, I picked up my Greek New Testament and began to dig deeper into the verse. What I discovered in that verse changed my life and set me free from worry, anxiety, fretting, and fear!

That night, I saw that the word "casting" used in First Peter 5:7 was the Greek word *epiripto*, a compound of the words *epi* and *ripto*. The word *epi* means upon, as on top of something. The word *ripto* means to hurl, to throw, or to cast, and it often means to violently throw or to fling something with great force.

The only other place this word *epiripto* is used in the New Testament is in Luke 19:35, where the Bible says, "And they brought him to Jesus: and they cast their garments upon the colt, and they set Jesus there on." It is important to note this passage, for it correctly conveys the idea of the word *epiripto*, which in secular literature often pictured the flinging of a garment, bag, or excess weight off the shoulders of a traveler and onto the back of some other beast, such as a donkey, camel, or horse.

We are not designed to carry the burden of worry, fretting, and anxiety. This load is simply too much for the human body and the central nervous system to tolerate. We may be able to manage it for a while, but eventually the physical body and mind will begin to break under this type of perpetual pressure. In fact, the medical world has confirmed that the major source of sickness in the Western Hemisphere is stress and pressure. Man was simply not fashioned to carry pressures, stresses, anxieties, and worries; this is the reason his body breaks down when it undergoes these negative influences for too long.

If you are struggling with sickness or depression, your condition very possibly could be related to stress and pressure. In First Peter 5:7, it is almost as if Jesus is calling out to you and saying, "Your shoulders are not big enough to carry the burdens you're trying to bear by yourself. This load will eventually break you — so please let ME be your beast of burden! Take that load and heave it with all your might. Fling it over onto MY back, and let ME carry it for you!" Just as Luke 19:35 says they cast their garments upon the back of the donkey, now you need to cast your burdens over on the Lord and let Him carry those burdens for you!

But exactly what problems and cares are we to throw over onto the shoulders of the Lord? The apostle Peter says we are to cast all of "our cares" upon Jesus. The word "cares" is the Greek word *merimna*, which means anxiety. However, in principle it describes any affliction, difficulty, hardship, misfortune, trouble, or complicated circumstance that arises as a result of problems that develop in our lives. It could refer to problems that are financial, marital, job-related, family-related, business-oriented, or anything else that concerns us.

This means anything that causes you worry or anxiety — regardless of why it happened — is what you need to throw over onto the shoulders of Jesus Christ! Nothing is too big or small to talk to the Lord about, Peter says, because He "careth for you." The word "careth" is taken from the Greek word *melei*, which means to be concerned; to be thoughtful; to be interested; to be aware; to notice; or to give painful and meticulous attention. Peter uses this word to assure us that Jesus really does care about us and the things that are heavy on our hearts. In fact, He gives meticulous attention to what is happening to us. He is interested in every facet of our lives.

So don't ever let the devil tell you that your problems are too stupid, small, or insignificant to bring to Jesus. The Lord is interested in everything that concerns you!

Because of the Greek words used in First Peter 5:7, this verse carries the following idea:

> *"Take that heavy burden, difficulty, or challenge you are carrying — the one that has arisen due to circumstances that have created hardship and struggles in your life — and fling those worries and anxieties over onto the back of the Lord! Let Him carry them for you! The Lord is extremely interested in every facet of your life and is genuinely concerned about your welfare."*

When I saw these Greek words and perceived how deeply Jesus cared about the burdens that were on my heart, I realized I was carrying a load I didn't have to bear by myself. Jesus was standing right at my side, longing to help me and inviting me to shift the weight from my shoulders to His shoulders. By faith, I heaved those financial cares onto the back of Jesus — and when I did, I was set free from the stress, anxiety, and pressure that had been weighing me down at that time in my life.

You don't have to carry the whole weight of the world by yourself. Jesus loves you so much and is so deeply concerned about you and the difficulties you are facing that He calls out to you today, "Roll those burdens over on Me. Let Me carry them for you so you can be free!"

If you are lugging around worries, cares, and concerns about your family, your business, your church, or any other area of your life, why not stop right now and say, "Jesus, I'm yielding every one of these concerns to You today. I cast my burden on You, and I thank You for setting me free!"

My Prayer for Today

Lord, I thank You for what I've read today. I regret having carried these burdens and worries so long by myself when, in fact, You were always ready to take them from me and to carry them on my behalf. But it's never too late to do what is right, so right now I make the decision to yield to You every one of these matters that are bothering me. Thank You for coming alongside me to take these weights from my shoulders. Because You are so loving and attentive to me, I can now go free!

I pray this in Jesus' name!

My Confession for Today

I confess that Jesus is standing right at my side, yearning to help me and inviting me to shift the weight from my shoulders to His shoulders so I can go free! By faith, I have already cast my cares onto Jesus. As a result, I am liberated from stress, anxiety, worries, pressures, and all the other things that have been bothering me!

I declare this by faith in Jesus' name!

Questions for You to Consider

1. Do you habitually worry and fret about certain things? What are the issues that weigh on your mind more than anything else?

_____

_____

_____

_____

_____

_____

2. Are you able to cast these cares over onto the Lord, or do you keep stirring yourself up with thoughts of fear, reigniting the fretting and the worry all over again even after you have already released those cares to the Lord?

_____

_____

_____

_____

_____

3. What triggers worry, fretting, and anxiety in you? Have you noticed key words, phrases, or events when worry and fretting begin to operate inside you? Recognizing those moments may help you prevent them from reoccurring, so consider well what kinds of situations arouse these emotions in you.

_____

_____

_____

_____

_____

Day 15

Two Kinds of Strongholds

> *(For the weapons of our warfare are not carnal, but mighty through God to the pulling down of strong holds;) casting down imaginations....*
>
> — **2 Corinthians 10:4,5**

If you want to be free from every stronghold of the enemy in your life, you have to understand that there are two kinds of strongholds: rational and irrational. The rational strongholds are the more difficult to deal with — because they usually make sense!

Paul refers to these rational strongholds when he says, "Casting down imaginations...." The word "imaginations" is taken from the Greek word *logismos*, which is where we get the word "logic," as in "logical thinking." Thank God for a good, sound mind, but even a sound mind must be submitted to the sanctifying work of the Holy Spirit. Otherwise, your mind will develop a stronghold of natural reasoning that starts to dictate all kinds of lies to your life. I call these rational strongholds.

The reason I call them rational strongholds is that they are strongholds in the mind that make sense! You see, your logical mind will always try to talk you out of obeying God. In fact, if you don't take charge of your mind, it will begin to completely dominate and control your obedience to God. It will tell you that you can't afford to obey the Lord and that it isn't a good time to step out in faith. Your natural mind will come up with a whole host of logical reasons to explain why you shouldn't do what the Spirit of God is telling you to do.

Second, there are irrational strongholds. These primarily have to do with completely unrealistic fears and worries, such as a fear of contracting a terminal disease, a fear of dying early in life, an abnormal fear of rejection, and so forth. These types of irrational strongholds in the mind, emotions, and imagination will normally play their course and then dissipate. But if harassing thoughts persist in your mind and insist on controlling you mentally and emotionally, you must deal with them straightforwardly with the Word of God.

In Second Corinthians 10:5, Paul says, "Casting down imaginations, and every high thing that exalteth itself against the knowledge of God, and bringing into captivity every thought to the obedience of Christ." Notice that Paul doesn't say one thing about bringing the devil into captivity. Rather, he tells you to take every thought into captivity to the obedience of Christ.

The devil tries to invade your life through lies that he plants in your brain. If you don't take your thoughts captive, it will be just a matter of time before the devil starts using those lies to create mental and emotional strongholds for the purpose of keeping you in bondage. But if you take your thoughts captive, then your thoughts cannot take you captive!

Whether those strongholds are rational or irrational, you can take authority over them and cast them down! So quit listening to every ol' lie that devil tries to sink into your brain, and start taking those thoughts into captivity to the obedience of Christ! Pull down every mental or emotional stronghold in your life with the supernatural weapons of warfare God has given you!

My Prayer for Today

Lord, help me to see any area of my life that is dominated by rational or irrational strongholds. Forgive me for allowing the devil to sink his lies into my mind, and help me now to uproot and cast down every one of his lies. I know that Your Word will renew my mind to think in accordance with You, so I am asking You today to help me make Your Word a priority in my life!

I pray this in Jesus' name!

My Confession for Today

I boldly declare that my mind is free from the devil's lies! I think God's thoughts; I meditate on God's Word; and my brain is spot-free from the rational and irrational strongholds that Satan would like to plant inside me. Because of God's Word working in me, I am completely free!

I declare this by faith in Jesus' name!

Questions for You to Consider

1. Can you think of three areas in which the devil has tried to penetrate your mind and take you captive with ridiculous, irrational lies?

   _____

   _____

   _____

   _____

   _____

   _____

2. Can you identify times in your life when the devil has tried to seize control of your mind with logical, rational strongholds in order to keep you from stepping out to do what God has asked you to do?

   _____

   _____

   _____

   _____

   _____

3. What steps can you start taking right now to cast these thoughts down so you can get free of these lies and move forward with God's plan?

_____

_____

_____

_____

_____

_____

_____

Day 16

Are Worry and Anxiety Trying to Seize or Control You?

> *Be careful for nothing; but in every thing by prayer and supplication with thanksgiving let your requests be made known unto God.*
>
> **— Philippians 4:6**

Do you ever have moments when anxiety tries to creep up on you and seize your heart? I'm talking about those times when you are thrown into a state of panic about things that concern you — such as your family, your friendships, your business, or your finances. Very often, this state of panic is caused by the mere thought of a problem that doesn't even exist and is unlikely to ever come to pass. Nevertheless, the mere thought of this non-existent problem troubles you deeply. Soon you find yourself sinking into such a strong state of worry and anxiety that it literally takes you emotionally hostage!

An example would be a wife or mother who worries endlessly about the health of her husband or children. Although in reality, they are as healthy as can be, the devil constantly pounds the woman's mind with fear-filled thoughts about her loved ones getting sick or dying prematurely. This fear acts like a stranglehold that gradually chokes off her life, paralyzing her until she can no longer function normally in her daily responsibilities.

Or have you ever known a successful businessman who lives in constant terror that he is going to lose his money? I've known many such men. Their businesses were blessed, stable, and even expanding. But because the devil struck their minds with worry and anxiety about losing it all, they weren't able to enjoy the success God had given them. Instead of enjoying God's goodness and His many blessings in their lives, they often lived like beggars, afraid that if they used what they had, they might lose it. This is a strangling, choking fear that steals people's ability to enjoy what they possess.

Some people are so controlled by fear that they pray fretful prayers instead of faith-filled prayers. I must admit that I've had moments in my own life when I've prayed more out of fretfulness than out of faith. Have you ever had one of those times? Praying fretful prayers doesn't get you anything. It is non-productive praying. God does not respond to fretfulness; He responds to faith.

In Philippians 4:6, Paul says, "Be careful for nothing; but in everything by prayer and supplication with thanksgiving let your requests be made known unto God." Do you see the word "careful" in this verse? It is the Greek word *merimnao*, which means to be troubled; to be anxious; to be fretful; or to be worried about something.

In New Testament times, this word was primarily used in connection with worry about finances, hunger, or some other basic provision of life. It pictured a person who is fretful about paying his bills; a person who is worried he won't have the money to purchase food and clothes for his family's needs or pay his house payment or apartment rent on time; or a person who is anxious about his ability to cope with the daily necessities of life.

This is the same word used in Matthew 6:25, when Jesus says, "Therefore I say unto you, Take no thought for your life, what ye shall eat, or what ye shall drink...." The word "thought" is also the Greek word *merimnao*. But in this particular verse, the Greek New Testament also has the word *me*, which is a strong prohibition to stop something that is already in progress.

This strongly suggests that Jesus was speaking to worriers who were already filled with fret and anxiety. He was urging these people to stop worrying. The verse could be translated, "Stop worrying about your life...." Then Jesus specifies that they were to stop worrying about "...what ye shall eat, or what ye shall drink...." So again, we see the word *merimnao* used to describe worry, fretfulness, and anxiety about obtaining the basic necessities of life.

We also find the word *merimnao* used in the parable of the sower and the seed. Matthew 13:22 says, "He also that received seed among the thorns is he that heareth the word; and the care of this world, and the deceitfulness of riches, choke the word, and he becometh unfruitful." The word "care" is the Greek word *merimnao*, again connected to material worries and concerns.

Jesus says such worry "chokes" the Word. The word "choke" is the Greek word *sumpnigo*, which means to suffocate; to smother; to asphyxiate; to choke; or to throttle. You see, worry is so all-consuming in an individual's mind that it literally chokes him. It is a suffocating, smothering force that throttles his whole life to a standstill.

In Luke 21:34, Jesus gives a special warning to people who live in the last days. He said, "And take heed to yourselves, lest at any time your hearts be overcharged with surfeiting, and drunkenness, and cares of this life, so that day come upon you unawares."

When Jesus mentions the "cares of this life," the word "cares" is the Greek word *merimna*. This time, however, it is used in connection with the word "life," which is the Greek word *biotikos*. This comes from the root word *bios*, the Greek word for life. It is where we get the word biology. But when it becomes the word *biotikos*, it describes the things of life — pertaining primarily to the events, incidents, and episodes that occur in one's life.

Thus, this phrase could be understood to mean that we should not allow ourselves to worry and fret about the events, incidents, or episodes that occur in life. This is a particularly fitting message for people who live in the last days and who are confronted by the incidents and episodes that occur during this difficult time.

So, when the apostle Paul writes in Philippians 4:6, "Be careful for nothing...," he is pleading with us not to be worried about the basic needs and provisions required for life. Paul is also telling us not to let the events of life get to us and throw us into a state of anxiety or panic. To let us know how free of all worry we should be, Paul says we are to be "careful for nothing." The word "nothing" is the Greek word *meden*, and it means absolutely nothing!

So this phrase in Philippians 4:6 could be translated:

"Don't be worried about anything — and that means nothing at all!"

So, what is bothering you today, friend? What is stealing your peace and joy? Is there one particular thing Satan keeps using to strike your mind with fear? Can you think of a single time when worry and fretfulness ever helped make a situation better? Doesn't worry serve only to keep you emotionally torn up and in a state of panic?

I urge you to put an end to worry today, once and for all. If you let worry start operating in you even for a moment, it will try to become a habitual part of your thought life, turning you into a "worrier" who never knows a moment of peace.

Jesus is sitting at the right hand of the Father right now, interceding for you continually. Jesus understands every emotion, every frustration, and every temptation you could ever face (*see* Hebrews 2:18). So why not make a deliberate decision to turn over all your worries to Jesus today? Rather than trying to manage those anxieties and needs all by yourself, go to Him and surrender everything into His loving, capable hands. Walk free of all those choking, paralyzing fears once and for all.

Jesus is waiting for you to cast all your cares upon Him, because He really does care for you (*see* 1 Peter 5:7). Then once you throw your worries and concerns on Him, He will help you experience the joy and peace He has designed for you to enjoy in life all along!

My Prayer for Today

Lord, I admit that I've allowed fear, worry, fretfulness, and anxiety to play a role in my life. When these negative emotions operate in me, I lose my peace and my joy. I am tired of living in this continual state of worry and fear about bad things that might happen. Jesus, today I am making the choice to turn all these destructive thoughts over to You. I don't want to live this way anymore. I know this isn't Your plan for my life, so by faith, I cast all my concerns on You. I release them into Your hands, Lord, and ask You to take them right now!

I pray this in Jesus' name!

My Confession for Today

I confess that I am free from worry, fretfulness, and anxiety. These forces have no place in me. I have surrendered every care and concern to Jesus, and He has taken them from me. As a result, I am free of every burden, every weight, and every problem. Jesus is my great High Priest, and He is interceding for me right now. With God on my side, I can enjoy life as He intended for me to enjoy it. I boldly confess that I am fear-free and worry-free, and that anxiety has no place in me!

I declare this by faith in Jesus' name!

Questions for You to Consider

1. What is the one area in your life where Satan most often strikes your mind and emotions with fear, fretfulness, and anxiety? Do you know what triggers this attack of fear and worry?

   _____

   _____

   _____

   _____

   _____

   _____

2. For you to get out of fear and to walk in peace, what steps do you need to take in your life? In other words, in order to move into a place of constant peace, what do you need to do differently than you're doing right now?

   _____

   _____

   _____

   _____

   _____

   _____

3. If you were going to counsel someone else who was being held hostage by worry, fretfulness, and anxiety, what would you tell that person to do to get free and to stay free?

_____

_____

_____

_____

_____

_____

Day 17

Possessing a Trouble-Free Heart

> *...Let not your heart be troubled, neither let it be afraid.*
>
> — John 14:27

I'll never forget the day waves of panic rolled through me as we were reconstructing a big building as a permanent home for our church in Moscow. Paying for the building had itself already required the most miraculous level of faith I had ever experienced. When we started the project, we estimated what it would cost to reconstruct the facility. However, we didn't know at the beginning of the process that the floors and columns of the entire building would have to be reinforced to hold the weight of the balcony we were adding to the building.

When I learned of the additional costs associated with reinforcing the floors and columns, a sense of panic surged through my whole being. Alarm, dread, horror — all these words could describe the emotions that tried to grip my soul.

Within seconds, I felt cold sweat and heat simultaneously flushing across my face, neck, ears, and upper chest. It felt like I had to somehow get hold of myself, or I would fall to pieces.

There was one thing I knew in that moment: allowing panic to get hold of me was not going to change the situation! So, I politely excused myself from the meeting where the facts and figures were being presented to me, and I took a walk by myself to catch my breath and bring my soul into submission before fearful emotions could wreak havoc with my peace.

As we proceeded to move forward on that building project, I had to face those same tumultuous emotions more than once. Taking a walk by myself to bring my soul into submission became a very familiar practice en route to completing that project. During those times, I learned to turn to Jesus' words in John 14:27, where He said, "...Let not your heart be troubled, neither let it be afraid." These words proved to be of great comfort to me in those times when my soul was tempted to give way to fear and trepidation.

As I'm sure you personally know, there is perhaps nothing more tormenting than to go through your daily life with a troubled heart. It can make you wallow in tumultuous feelings of worry, inadequacy, or regret. It can tear you up emotionally and steal your joy. And when fear is added to the mix, it can escalate your troubled state to an even higher level of anxiety. That's why it's so important that you take Jesus' words deep into your heart that you do not ever have to live with a troubled and fearful heart.

Jesus said, "...Let not your heart be troubled, neither let it be afraid" (John 14:27). The word "troubled" is the Greek word *taresso*, which is used in various places in the New Testament to mean to shake; to trouble; to disquiet; to unsettle; to perplex; to cause anxiety; or even to cause feelings of grief. It is the picture of someone feeling inwardly shaken, unsettled, confused, and upset. If you've felt that way, you know exactly what I mean!

Often when these troubling emotions begin to work in the soul, they open the door to other negative emotions and eventually pull you over into the realm of fear. That's why it is so important to bring the soul into submission before this happens. This is precisely why Jesus continued to say, "Let not your heart be troubled, neither let it be afraid."

The word "afraid" is from a form of the word *deiliao*, and depicts a gripping fear or dread that produces a shrinking back or cowardice. In essence, it saps your ability to look at the problem head-on and causes you to retreat into your own mode of self-preservation — which, in effect, is cowardice or the lack of courage to face what is before you.

This word *deiliao* is also a form of the Greek word that Paul used in Second Timothy 1:7 when he told Timothy, "God has not given us the spirit of fear; but of power, and of love, and of a sound mind." Timothy was facing real problems at the time Paul wrote this verse to him. His problems were not imaginary. Nevertheless, Paul didn't want Timothy's emotions to be in bondage to a spirit of fear that would turn him into a coward. Shrinking back from reality wouldn't help the younger minister or anyone else involved in the situation. So, Paul told Timothy that his being subject to a sense of fear or panic was not the will of God, for the Lord had given him spiritual equipment of an entirely different nature — a spirit of power, love, and a sound mind!

With this in mind, look again at the words of Jesus in John 14:27, which can convey this idea:

> *"Don't let your heart be torn up by things that unsettle you, neither let it be taken with fear that causes you to shrink back into cowardice."*

How well Jesus understands what you and I are facing! We were not created to be torn up in our emotions! That's why we must quickly learn to grab hold of our emotions and tell ourselves, I wasn't made for this! I refuse to allow this sense of panic and fear to get hold of me! Jesus is Lord over every situation I commit to Him, and that includes the one I'm looking at right now!

In moments when fear has tried to grip me, and I admit it has happened multiple times over the years, I've learned to run to John 14:27 and to rehearse the words of Jesus to myself over and over again. Jesus knows us. He knew what we'd be facing in life, so He instructed us in advance on how to deal with it!

Allowing yourself to stay in a state of feeling troubled, upset, and fearful won't help you in life. In fact, it will hinder you in running the race God has set before you! So, take Jesus' words very seriously and refuse to let your heart be troubled. Jesus wouldn't tell you to do something you couldn't do, so you can know that you are well able to make that choice!

Don't allow yourself to yield to fear in any form. You have the spirit of power and love and a sound mind working in you. That means you are well able to grab hold of any negative emotions and pull them in line with God's Word, even in a situation that challenges you to the core. You can just settle it for yourself today: You are not of those who shrink back (*see* Hebrews 10:39). No, you're among those who bring their souls into submission to God's Word and live as overcomers in this life!

My Prayer for Today

Father, I acknowledge that I've allowed myself to get into a troubled state of heart and soul. Circumstances have left me feeling shaken and upset, and I haven't dealt with those feelings according to the Word. As a result, a door was opened to a spirit of fear that is now trying to call the shots in my life. I repent, because it is sin for me not to trust You, and I ask You to please forgive me for allowing these negative emotions to find a place to take up residence in my life. So, now I open my heart for the Holy Spirit to infuse me with the power I need to take authority over the spirit of fear and tell it to leave me once and for all.

I pray this in Jesus' name!

My Confession for Today

I confess that my heart, mind, and emotions are not made to be a refuge for fear and intimidation to take up residence in me and torment me. I refuse to nurse these negative emotions any longer or to let them operate inside my soul! I have tolerated fear too long! I refuse to retreat into a toxic state of isolation and self-preservation. God has too many things for me to do in this life to waste a moment in torment and fear, so I'm moving forward by faith to defeat the enemy's strategy against me today. I do it in the power of the Holy Spirit and with the name of Jesus!

I declare this by faith in Jesus' name!

Questions for You to Consider

1. Can you think of an experience when a spirit of fear tried to grab hold of you? What did you do to break its grip on your soul?

_____

_____

_____

_____

_____

_____

2. If you had a friend who was being torn up emotionally and mentally by a spirit of fear, what would you advise that friend to do? Have you taken this advice for yourself?

_____

_____

_____

_____

_____

_____

3. Do you know someone who is dealing with a troubled heart or being tormented by thoughts of fear right now? What should you do to help that person get victory over that situation?

_____

_____

_____

_____

_____

_____

Day 18

How Will You Respond to Negative Situations?

> *There hath no temptation taken you but such as is common to man....*
>
> — 1 Corinthians 10:13

Have you ever noticed that the more you focus on a problem, the bigger and more intense it seems to become? In fact, if you don't get a grip on your emotions in these situations, your mind will try to blow that problem far out of proportion. Even if you're facing a real crisis, you have the power to get your mind under control with help from the Holy Spirit. However, if you let your emotions have their way, they will play the worst-case scenario over and over in your mind until it finally manifests as a reality in your life.

That's why it is so important to decide beforehand how you're going to respond to negative situations! Instead of blowing them out of proportion, you can make the decision before anything bad even happens that you and the Holy Spirit are bigger and stronger than any problem that will ever come your way. The two of you together, armed with the all-powerful name of Jesus, can tackle and overcome anything that ever comes against you! Plus, if you are blessed to have one or two friends who can encourage you in the Word or with agreement in prayer, you have everything to shout about!

The principle is precisely the same when dealing with temptations. All temptations begin as thoughts in the mind. They might appeal to your flesh, but each one of them first takes form in the mind and emotions. In the beginning, those thoughts are manageable, conquerable, and even rejectable. If you'll just change your focus, get out of the situation, and minimize it in your mind by refusing to focus on it, you can leave that temptation in the dust.

Or, if you feel that you're losing the battle alone, you can open your heart to a faithful friend and ask for help. With the power of the Holy Spirit and a dear friend at your side, every temptation can really be downplayed, minimized, and conquered!

I like how the apostle Paul taught about this in First Corinthians 10:13. He said, "There hath no temptation taken you but such as is common to man...." The word "temptation" is very fierce in the Greek language. It's the word *peirasmos*, and it depicts that moment when we feel seized and squeezed by eternal or internal forces that are designed to take us down. But these feelings are momentary and relatively powerless according to Paul. It's all a masquerade of flesh merely trying to act powerful. Paul described these as being "common to man."

The phrase "common to man" is a translation of the Greek word *anthropinos*, which describes things that are normally experienced by human beings and are therefore not exceptional. Rather than blow these temptations out of proportion,

Paul downplayed them as being commonplace. Furthermore, he continued by saying that God "...with the temptation will make a way to escape..." (1 Corinthians 10:13). If these temptations were truly overpowering, they would be inescapable. However, Paul clearly stated that we can easily escape them.

The word "escape" is the Greek word *ekbasis*, which is a compound of the words *ek* and *basis*. The word *ek* simply means out, and the word *basis* means to step. When these two words are compounded, the new word *ekbasis* means to step out. In other words, you can walk away from or step out of a temptation just as easily as you walked into one.

It's all a matter of what you believe.

The devil will always try to convince you that you are a tiny, powerless being with no authority to withstand his lies. If you take his bait, you'll have a very difficult time walking away from the temptations that assail your mind. Instead, you can choose to think like Paul and say, "These silly temptations are nothing special that human beings haven't faced many times. There is nothing powerful or special about them, and I will walk away from these emotions." As you do, you'll find your stance of authority in Christ has increased in strength, and the mental drama you used to experience from those negative thoughts will become negligible!

Decide beforehand how you're going to respond to negative thoughts! You have to make the decision to believe that you and the Holy Spirit are bigger and stronger than any problem that will ever come your way. With Jesus on your side, you can look at those temptations and declare, "You do not have authority over me! You are nothing more than a simple human temptation that has affected millions of people through history before me, and there are legions of people who have resisted and defeated you. And today I am being added to the number of those who say NO to you! I refuse to let this temptation become a drama! I am picking up my feet and walking away from your voice. In the name of Jesus, you have no more authority over me!"

My Prayer for Today

Father, I thank You for the truth of Your Word. I allow it to transform me into a new person by changing the way I think. Anytime I feel seized and squeezed by external or internal forces designed to take me down, help me remember that there is no temptation that is not common to man. With every temptation that presents itself, You also present the way of escape from it.

I pray this in Jesus' name!

My Confession for Today

I declare that I make the decision to leave temptation in the dust. I choose to magnify the Lord and minimize every attempt to lure and appeal to my flesh through temptation in any form. I am not powerless or without authority and strength. I stand strong in the boldness, authority, and strength of God by the power of His Spirit within me. Because I am born of God, I am an overcomer in this life! Knowing that Jesus Christ Himself and countless others have resisted and defeated the very same temptation, I choose to walk away from these silly temptations and the emotions that surround them! The Holy Spirit in me is bigger than any temptation that tries to come against me — I can simply walk away from it!

I declare this by faith in Jesus' name!

Questions for You to Consider

1. Can you think of a temptation or thought that has tried to habitually keep you down and depressed? What do you think about it now after reading today's lesson? Do you still think this thought or temptation holds power over you, or do you think that you've just been hoodwinked by the devil in this respect?

_____

_____

_____

_____

_____

2. You've said no to many things in the past — what is keeping you from lifting your voice and exercising your authority right now? Is it that you enjoy the sin? Be honest!

_____

_____

_____

_____

_____

3. Can you honestly say you're facing something more insurmountable than the power of God can overcome? Why don't you dig your heels in the ground, tell the devil to hit the road, throw up your arms, and start rejoicing that this particular temptation has no right to exercise itself over you any longer?

_____

_____

_____

_____

_____

_____

Day 19

Choose to Let It Go!

> *Forbearing one another, and forgiving one another, if any man have a quarrel against any: even as Christ forgave you, so also do ye.*
>
> — **Colossians 3:13**

Every day we encounter opportunities to get upset with people about something they did or said. If we let down our guard and indulge in these urges, we will live in a continual state of frustration and strife, and our spiritual lives will suffer dramatically. Sometimes it can be very difficult to convince our minds to overlook a perceived slight, forgive the offender, and move on with our lives. However, the Bible offers us a powerful strategy that can be used to cultivate peace in our relationships: We must learn to extend grace to others and to realize that humans act human.

In Colossians 3:13, the apostle Paul wrote, "Forbearing one another, and forgiving one another, if any man have a quarrel against any: even as Christ forgave you, so also do ye." This verse specifically outlines how we are to respond to people in our lives who disappoint or upset us. And since life is filled with disappointments, it's important for us to understand exactly what Paul meant when he wrote these words.

Paul began with the phrase, "Forbearing one another...." This word "forbearing" is from the Greek word *anechomai*, which means to endure one another, to put up with one another, or to have tolerance of one another. It is the opposite of acting intolerant or being short-tempered with other people. At some point along the way, we all become frustrated with our friends, family, coworkers, and acquaintances. In those moments, the most Christ-like attitude to demonstrate may be to simply show forbearance and let it go. That doesn't mean we have to compromise or ignore an obvious problem; however, it does mean that sometimes taking the higher road means shutting our mouths and letting go of the offense or disappointment.

That's why Paul said in this verse that sometimes forbearing or putting up with the people you interact with in life is the highest road you can take. So when your flesh gets offended, or you find yourself wanting to nitpick someone about what you perceive to be his or her failures, take some time to get quiet before God and ask Him what to do. It may be that His highest will in that situation is for you to simply show forbearance and let go of the matter. Although loving confrontation is needed at times, it is not always the right course to take.

Paul went on to say, "Forbearing one another, and forgiving one another...." The word "forgiving" comes from the word *charis*, the Greek word for grace. It carries the idea of wholeheartedly forgiving, freely forgiving, or readily forgiving. This is a step beyond simply being forbearing; it requires our response to go to the next level as we choose to freely and wholeheartedly forgive with no restraints and no strings attached. Just as God has extended His grace to us so many times by freely forgiving us of our sins against Him, now the Holy Spirit instructs you and me to extend forgiveness to those who have wronged us or offended us.

In the latter part of this verse, Paul relayed the core of his message, saying, "...If any man have a quarrel against any, even as Christ forgave you, so also do ye." The word "quarrel" is a Greek word *mamphe*, which means a complaint or grievance against someone and usually depicts a complaint that is backed with solid evidence.

Perhaps someone failed to do what you expected him to do or acted in a manner that was below your expectations of him. Regardless of what you perceive that this person did wrong or what "quarrel" you have with him, the Bible commands you to forgive "even as Christ forgave you." Isn't that what Christ did for you?

It's difficult for me to imagine why any of us would refuse to forgive someone else for a perceived offense in light of how graciously God has forgiven us. Certainly, we are all guilty or worthy of blame! How could we ever forget that it was for our dreadful sin that Jesus died on the Cross? Jesus bore unspeakable suffering by taking on punishment He didn't deserve — and He did it freely for us.

Now Paul urged us, "...As Christ forgave you, so also do ye." You and I didn't deserve the forgiveness we received, but God forgave us anyway. He forgave us for all we have done in the past, and His mercy is so boundless that He continues to forgive us in the present when we ask for forgiveness. Now we who are forgiven have a responsibility to forgive.

So if you're having a day filled with opportunities to get upset with people and you feel yourself sliding into a state of frustration and strife, take a moment to pause and meditate on the truths of Colossians 3:13. When you remember how much you've been forgiven by Christ — and by others whom you've deliberately or accidentally wronged in the past — you'll realize you don't have a right to stay upset with anyone!

My Prayer for Today

Father, I repent for allowing myself to become angry, frustrated, and unforgiving. That is wrong, and I refuse to yield to selfishness any longer. No matter what has been said or done, I have no right to harbor ill will — especially when You have commanded me to forgive others as You have forgiven me. Jesus, You paid a horrific price for my sins. Even as You hung dying on the Cross at Calvary, You prayed not only for me but also for the person I'm upset with now. Lord, I deeply apologize. If I had been focused on You instead of myself, I would not have become upset in the first place. Help me to see this person and this situation through Your eyes. I choose to get over this offense right now. I let this drop, and I refuse to think on my feelings anymore. Instead, I will seek to honor You in this matter. Holy Spirit, teach me how to love as Jesus loved me.

I pray this in Jesus' name!

My Confession for Today

I confess that I take heed to myself and I refuse to walk in unforgiveness, bitterness, or strife. I cannot control what others may say or do, but I am responsible for the condition of my own heart. I do not give place to the devil by indulging selfish thoughts or emotions. Neither do I attempt to justify my own negative behavior in response to what upset me. Instead, I choose to give place to the love of God, which is shed abroad in my heart by the Holy Spirit who indwells me. And I make a daily decision to love and to forgive others as God through Christ has loved and forgiven me.

I declare this by faith, in Jesus' name!

Questions for You to Consider

1. Can you think of someone you wronged, intentionally or unin-tentionally, but regardless of your bad behavior, they took the high road and forgave you for it?

   _____

   _____

   _____

   _____

   _____

   _____

2. Maybe you have a personal quarrel with someone right now and can even claim to have evidence to back up your position. But is it really worth the lack of peace that it's creating in your life? Is this a fight you should be fighting, or would it be more produc-tive to just let it go and forget about it?

   _____

   _____

   _____

   _____

   _____

   _____

3. Have you had other instances in your life when you got upset with someone and held on to it for a long time, but then you finally woke up and realized it wasn't worth the lack of peace, so you decided to forgive? How much precious time was wasted that could never be recaptured because you got upset? Have you considered that this may be something you're going through right now? Why don't you choose forgiveness, move on, and let the Lord deal with it in His own way?

_____

_____

_____

_____

_____

Day 20

Kick Back and Take a Breather Every Once in a While!

> *And to you who are troubled rest with us, when the Lord Jesus shall be revealed from heaven with his mighty angels.*
>
> — 2 Thessalonians 1:7

Whether we like it or not, there are moments when we run into troubling times in our lives. The trouble may arise in our job, our marriage, our children, our finances, or some other area of our lives. It can feel like there is no let-up from the constant, never-ending grind of what is happening to us. Although we can take this kind of nonstop pressure for a while, eventually it becomes too much if there is no let-up from it, and we begin to feel like we're going to collapse from the burden we're carrying.

If we walk in the Spirit, we can avoid many pitfalls that the devil and life try to throw our way. But the truth is, as long as we are in the world — where the devil actively seeks to kill, steal, and destroy — there will be troubles from time to time in our lives. Therefore, we need to know how to respond when we feel like we are being assaulted by nonstop problems, and there seems to be no let-up or relief from the stress we're experiencing.

I remember a time in Moscow when I was battling enemies on every front. Because our church was rapidly growing, we were in perpetual need of more finances. In addition, we had been kicked out of several auditoriums by local authorities and were about to be kicked out again. I felt like we were spending our lives searching high and low for an auditorium that would accommodate our growing church, but to no avail. We couldn't seem to find another auditorium for our church meetings, and time was running out. I felt like I was at the end of my rope!

I lay in my bed night after night, asking God to help us find a solution to these problems. Finally, Denise said to me, "Rick, you need to get away and take a break from all this!"

I asked her, "How can I take a break when we are in such a tight jam? How can I get away right now when we're facing so many challenges?"

She answered, "If you'll get away and rest a little — if you'll step back from these all-consuming problems — your thoughts will clear up. It will be easier to see the situation from God's perspective so you can receive the wisdom you need from Him."

I remember thinking how irresponsible it would be for me to get away during such a time of difficulty. But I was studying my Bible at that moment, and just then I saw something in Second Thessalonians 1:7 I had never seen before. Paul told the Thessalonians, "And to you who are troubled rest with us...." When I saw that word "rest," I reached for my Greek New Testament to look it up — and was I ever blessed when I saw what it meant!

Before I tell you what I discovered that day, let me first give you a little bit of background about what was happening to the Thessalonian church at the time the apostle Paul wrote this verse to them.

Paul and his apostolic team first preached the Gospel in Thessalonica and subsequently established the church there (*see* Acts 17:1-9). It was during this time that he and his team laid the first foundations for a church that would eventually challenge the forces of paganism and the hatred of the Jews. The opposition from the Jews became so intense and violent that they were driven from the city and fled to Berea (*see* Acts 17:10).

Because of the spiritual, religious, and political environment in Thessalonica, the intensity of persecution there was terrific — among the most outrageous demonstrations of persecution that occurred while the New Testament Church was being established. Although these believers were submitted to pounding pressures from outside forces, they refused to surrender to defeat. Day after day, they lived, breathed, and functioned without relief within this climate of extreme persecution and pressure. That is why Paul told them, "And to you who are troubled rest with us...."

The word "troubled" in this verse was a favorite word with Paul when he described the difficult events he and his team encountered in ministry. It is the Greek word *thlipsis* — a word so strong that it leaves no room for the intensity of these persecutions to be misunderstood. It conveys the idea of a heavy-pressure situation. One scholar says it was first used to describe the specific act of tying a victim with a rope, laying him on his back, and then placing a huge boulder on top of him until his body was crushed. Paul used this word to alert us to moments when he or others went through grueling, crushing situations that would have been unbearable, intolerable, and impossible to survive if it had not been for the help of the Holy Spirit.

Then Paul went on to say, "To those of you who are troubled rest with us...." The word "rest" is the Greek word *anesis*, which means to let up, to relax, to stop being stressed, or to find relief. One scholar notes that it was used in the secular Greek world to denote the release of a bowstring that has been under great pressure. It was also used figuratively to mean relaxation from the stresses of life or freedom to have a little recreation. In this case, Paul was urging the Thessalonians to find relief from the constant stress they were undergoing as a result of opposition to their faith. Paul exhorted them to let it go, shake it off, and learn how to find relief, even in the midst of difficult circumstances.

An interpretive translation of Second Thessalonians 1:7 could read:

> *"To you who are going through difficulties right now, it's time for you to let up, take a breather, and relax. We know what it's like to be under constant pressure, but no one can stay under that kind of stress continuously. So join us in learning how to loosen up a bit. Shake off your troubles, and allow yourself a little relaxation and time for recreation."*

When I saw these Greek words in this verse, I told my wife, "You're right! I need a break from all these troubles — and here's a scripture that confirms it! It tells me I need to loosen up and allow myself a little time for relaxation and recreation."

So, I took time away from the office, refused to talk about work, and simply allowed myself to enjoy a few days with no pressure. And when I returned to work, I found that I could clearly see the answer I had been struggling to find.

If you feel depleted and fatigued, is it possible that you need to get away for a little while? Could it be that the Lord is urging you to take a breather from the constant pace you're maintaining so you can shake off the problems and relax a little bit? Don't you agree that when you're under constant pressure, it affects your ability to think right and see things clearly? Now you have a Scripture to back you up when you need to get alone with the Lord to pray and worship Him — or simply allow yourself some time for recreation. And don't feel guilty about it — it's the recommendation of the apostle Paul himself!

We live in a world that is spinning faster and faster, so we have to learn how to keep our lives in balance so we can keep our focus clear. So why don't you start putting a little time aside for yourself so you can shake off the problems that are trying to steal your joy today!

My Prayer for Today

Lord, I ask for wisdom to know how to balance my life and work with times of relaxation and recreation. I am tempted to work nonstop and never take a break, and as a result, I get tired and worn out. Forgive me for not taking better care of myself. I yield to Your peace, and I resist the feelings of guilt that try to overwhelm me when I am away from my work and responsibilities. I now know that You want me to take a break from this constant pace and learn to relax a little. Holy Spirit, I thank You for helping me make this change in my life.

I pray this in Jesus' name!

My Confession for Today

I confess that I live my life in balance! I work hard, but I also set aside time for my mind and my body to be refreshed. God's Word declares that I need to take a breather from time to time, so I do it obediently and joyfully with no feelings of guilt or condemnation. God expects me to work hard, but He also expects me to be recharged and refilled! I am making a change in my life so I can include time to be revitalized and refreshed!

I declare this by faith in Jesus' name!

Questions for You to Consider

1. Do you give yourself a little time for rest and relaxation, or do you feel guilty when you are not always working?

_____

_____

_____

_____

_____

_____

2. Can you think of a time when you worked so hard that you nearly depleted yourself of strength, and when you took a little time off and rested, you came back to work refreshed, refilled, and recharged?

_____

_____

_____

_____

_____

_____

3. When you are tired and need a break from your regular schedule, what do you do for that scheduled time of rest? What are some things you could do to make sure you have your needed time of refreshment?

_____

_____

_____

_____

_____

_____

Day 21

Making Time for Prayer

> *And straightway he [Jesus] constrained his disciples to get into the ship, and to go to the other side before unto Bethsaida, while he sent away the people. And when he had sent them away, he departed into a mountain to pray.*
>
> **— Mark 6:45,46**

When taking stock of the monumental issues facing the world today, many believers are tempted to succumb to worry, stress, and anxiety. However, living in a mental prison of fear and anxiety is not God's plan for your life. As a child of God, you can find peace no matter what storm is raging all around you! Psalm 55:22 states, "Cast thy burden upon the Lord, and he shall sustain thee: he shall never suffer the righteous to be moved." According to this verse, the way to remain in peace is to spend concentrated time in the presence of the Lord.

Setting time aside to get quiet and seek God so you can hear His voice can be a challenge for busy people. Personally, I am the type of person who loves to be on the go all the time, and there have been times in my life when I neglected to take enough time to be quiet before the Lord. However, a few years ago, He spoke to my heart and called me aside for a special, intense time of prayer and seeking His face. I am so thankful that I heeded His call because that time with God opened my heart so He could show me the areas of my life that required change. During that special time of prayer, I pored over the Scriptures, and as I studied, I found there were many examples in the Bible of believers who sensed a "calling away." Moreover, I found that each person who obeyed this call to prayer and separated himself for a time of seeking the Lord received divine blessings as a result.

Even Jesus had times when He withdrew from the daily schedule of life to give Himself to consecrated times of prayer. An example can be found in Mark 6:45 and 46, which says, "And straightway he [Jesus] constrained his disciples to get into the ship, and to go to the other side before unto Bethsaida, while he sent away the people. And when he had sent them away, he departed into a mountain to pray."

Prior to the events described in this verse, Jesus had just miraculously fed 5,000 people, concluded one of the largest meetings of His ministry, and built momentum and excitement among His followers. In fact, the entire region was buzzing about the miracle of providing supernatural food for the entire multitude. But how did Jesus respond to this astounding event? He told the disciples to get on a ship and sail away; He sent away the crowds; and then He headed for the mountains to pray!

I want you to notice the word "straightway" in Mark 6:45. This word is a translation of the Greek word *eutheos*, which carries the idea of doing something without any delays, intervening circumstances, or detours. This word speaks both to the timing and the determination of Jesus. His response to a great victory was to withdraw without delay or interruption and get to a place where He could pray to the Father without interference. Jesus sent away the disciples and the multitude so that He might have time alone with God.

Next, notice the word "constrained" in the same verse. This is the Greek word *anagkazo*, which is a compound of the two words *ana* and *agkale*. *Ana* means up, and *agkale* means arm. When compounded, the new word paints the picture of a raised arm, which demonstrates force and authority. It literally means to compel by force. In light of the miracle that had just occurred in Jesus' ministry, I am amazed by the Gospel writer's choice of these two words "straightway" and "constrained" because it illustrates exactly how Jesus responded to that great meeting: He immediately — with determined force — caused everyone to leave Him alone so that He could pray!

With so much work to be done in our own ministry, I frequently feel compelled to just keep going strong without a break. But that is not what Jesus did. He recognized His need to stay in touch with the Father, even in the midst of successful events. And it's interesting to note that it was after His time with the Father that Jesus walked on the water and commanded a storm to be still (*see* Mark 6:47-51). I want to follow Jesus' example.

Anyone who knows Denise and me and is familiar with our ministry knows that we believe wholeheartedly in working very hard and giving 100 percent to the call of God. But there is a time when each of us must come aside to spend special time with the Lord and press into His presence so He can refresh us and renew us by His Spirit, just as Jesus did after He fed the multitude. So, I have determined to carve out special time with the Father — to pray, to read His Word, and to fellowship with Him. I set aside time just for Him so He can search my heart and change me and so I can hear Him speak to me with no distractions and interruptions.

I know many people are facing struggles right now, and maybe this is a hard time for you as well. The only way you will get through this time victoriously is by spending time with the Lord and casting the weight of all your cares on Him (*see* Psalm 55:22). Isn't it time for you to give God more time than you've been giving Him?

If God is calling you to set aside some extra time for Him, you need to be prepared for your flesh to put up a fight! That's why it's going to take determination to do it. When other things try to scream for your attention and pull you out of that consecrated place, you have to be determined to stay there unmoved, because that is where your source of strength, your peace, and all your answers will come from.

So, obey what the Holy Spirit tells you to do by going to your mountain to be with the Father — in other words, by coming aside every day to spend special time with Him. I guarantee you that your obedience will bring a great reward. As the author of Hebrews declares, "...He is a rewarder of them that diligently seek him" (Hebrews 11:6).

It is essential that you make a deliberate effort to regularly spend time in consecrated prayer. Start this week — start today. Start by giving Him at least a few more minutes each day. Then let your special time with the Lord grow and grow until you are finally experiencing quality time with God that surpasses anything you've ever known in your life. He will open your heart, remove the things that have troubled you and caused your defeat, refill you with the Holy Spirit, and give you joy unspeakable and full of glory!

My Prayer for Today

Father, with all that I have to do today, I cannot afford to miss spending time alone with You. I repent for the days I have sought to serve You in my own strength. I was busy, but not always fruitful because I failed to maintain my vital connection with You. Lord Jesus, I deliberately look to You, and I look away from all that would distract my attention from You. Father, I diligently seek You, and I thank You for rewarding me with a greater revelation of Your wisdom and Your ways. Holy Spirit, teach me to order my days with the Lord occupying first place. Please refill me today with Your power and Your joy, which is my impenetrable strength!

I pray this in Jesus' name!

My Confession for Today

I confess that I will daily spend time in the Father's presence. No matter how full my schedule may be, I will come to Him for direction and to be refreshed and renewed. I make God's Word my priority. I will not allow my flesh to lure me away from staying vitally united to the Vine because apart from Him, I know I can't do anything of eternal value. I set aside time to read the Word, pray, and fellowship with the Lord. I search my own heart on a regular basis and allow Him to change me so His anointing will flow pure and strong through my life.

I declare this by faith in Jesus' name!

Questions for You to Consider

1. Do you spend daily time with the Lord? How do you spend that time?

   _____

   _____

   _____

   _____

   _____

   _____

2. Do you have a daily Bible reading plan that helps you spend your time with the Lord? If not, a variety of reading plans are available online and are easy to find. Having a scheduled plan will help you feel like you do not have to figure it all out on your own.

   _____

   _____

   _____

   _____

   _____

   _____

3. I personally have a "place" where I go to read my Bible and pray. It has become my "mountain" where I retreat from the busyness of life to be with Jesus. Do you have such a place? Where is it?

_____

_____

_____

_____

_____

_____

Day 22

What Does It Mean to Have a 'Sound Mind'?

> *For God hath not given us the spirit of fear; but of power, and of love, and of a sound mind.*
>
> — **2 Timothy 1:7**

In moments of stress, pressure, or fear or when you're so exhausted you can't think straight, have you ever been tempted to say, "Dear God, what is wrong with me? I feel like I'm losing my mind"?

If you've ever felt this way before or if you're tempted to think like this right now, let me assure you: You're not going crazy! God's Word declares that you have been given a sound mind that works even in the craziest and most difficult situations!

Let me give you an example from the Bible. When Paul wrote the book of Second Timothy, it was a very difficult time for the Early Church. Due to

Nero's insanity, he was persecuting believers everywhere — and his methods of persecution were gruesome and cruel. At that time, Timothy was the pastor of the church of Ephesus. He knew that Nero's secret police would take special pleasure in killing him in some barbaric way if they ever got their hands on him.

As Timothy considered the threat against his life, a spirit of fear tried to grab hold of him. That's why Paul told Timothy in Second Timothy 1:7, "For God hath not given us the spirit of fear; but of power, and of love, and of a sound mind."

I want to especially point your focus to the words "sound mind." This phrase is taken from the Greek word *sophroneo*, which is a compound word combining *sodzo* and *phroneo*. The Greek word *sodzo* means to be saved or delivered. It suggests something that is delivered, rescued, revived, salvaged, and protected and is now safe and secure. One expositor suggests that the word *sodzo* could actually depict a person who was on the verge of death but then was revived and resuscitated because new life was breathed into him.

The second part of the phrase "sound mind" comes from the Greek word *phroneo*, which carries the idea of a person's intelligence or total frame of thinking — including his rationale, logic, and emotions. The word *phroneo* refers to every part of the human mind, including all the processes that are engaged in making the mind function and come to conclusions.

When the words *sodzo* and *phroneo* are compounded into one word, they form the word *sophroneo*, which pictures a mind that has been delivered, rescued, revived, salvaged, and protected and is now safe and secure. Thus, even if your mind is tempted to succumb to fear, as was the case with Timothy, you can allow God's Word and the Holy Spirit to work in you to deliver, rescue, revive, and salvage your mind. This means your rationale, logic, and emotions can be shielded from the illogically absurd, ridiculous, unfounded, and crazy thoughts that have tried to grip your mind in the past. All you have to do is grab hold of God's Word and His Spirit.

The word *sophroneo* in Second Timothy 1:7 could be translated:

> *"God has not given you a spirit of fear, but of power and of love —*
> *He has given you a mind that has been delivered, rescued, revived,*
> *salvaged, protected, and brought into a place of safety and security*
> *so that it is no longer affected by illogical, unfounded, and absurd*
> *thoughts."*

You see, when your mind is guarded by the Word of God, you think differently. When the Word of God is allowed to work in your mind, it safeguards your emotions; it defends your mind from demonic assault; and it shields you from arrows the enemy may try to shoot in your direction in order to arouse a spirit of fear inside you.

Why is it important for you to understand this? Because when you begin to live a life of faith — when you reach out to do the impossible — the enemy will try to assault you mentally and emotionally in an attempt to stop your progress. For instance, he may speak to your mind, saying things like, You can't do this! This doesn't make sense! Are you crazy?

So what do you do when the devil tries to convince you that you're losing your mind? What do you do if you're confused due to stressful situations and so tempted to fear that you can't think straight? Go get alone with the Lord and give Him your concerns. As you focus on Jesus and release all those burdens, you'll find that your mind is working fine! Second Timothy 1:7 promises you a sound mind; therefore, you have the right and privilege to tell the devil to shut up and then to declare by faith that your mind is sound, safe, and secure!

My Prayer for Today

Lord, I thank You by faith that I am NOT going crazy, and I am NOT losing my mind. The stress and pressure I've been facing is going to pass, and I know You will bring me through these challenging times. You promised me a sound mind, and that is exactly what You have given me. I can't ever thank You enough or fully express my gratitude for the power, love, and sound mind You have given to me that will carry me safely through these times!

I pray this in Jesus' name!

My Confession for Today

I declare that my mind is guarded by the Word of God. God's Word works in my mind; safeguards my emotions; defends my mind from demonic assault; and shields me from the arrows the enemy tries to shoot in my direction in order to arouse a spirit of fear inside me. When the devil tries to convince me that I'm losing my mind or to confuse me with stressful situations, I get alone with the Lord and give my concerns to Him. As I focus on Jesus and release all those burdens, I find that my mind is working fine!

I declare this by faith in Jesus' name!

Questions for You to Consider

1. Have you ever had a moment in your life when you were tempted to think that you were going crazy or that you were losing your mind?

    _____

    _____

    _____

    _____

    _____

    _____

2. What kind of circumstances were you facing in your life at that time?

    _____

    _____

    _____

    _____

    _____

    _____

3. What actions did you take during that difficult time that helped bring you back in touch with the "sound mind" that rightfully belongs to you?

_____

_____

_____

_____

_____

_____

Day 23

Rejuvenated by the Spirit of God!

> *But if the Spirit of him that raised up Jesus from the dead dwell in you, he that raised up Christ from the dead shall also quicken your mortal bodies by his Spirit that dwelleth in you.*
>
> — **Romans 8:11**

Recently I was thinking of the pressures and stresses that affect so many people's lives. People live their lives in their cars as they spend endless hours on expressways each day. They take their kids back and forth to school and to sports events; they go to church functions, to the grocery store, and back and forth to work. This constant movement puts a lot of stress on the mind and body. Yet there seems to be no option but to constantly try to keep up with the hectic pace!

Then when you finally get home in the evening, you can't really rest. After all, the bills must be paid; the house must be maintained; the yard needs mowing;

dishes need washing; dinner needs to be cooked; groceries have to be put away; the children need special attention and discipline. Walking through the door of the house at the end of the workday does not mean your work is finished. You have switched to a different kind of work.

Then there are still church responsibilities. You want to be faithful to your church and serve in as many areas as possible. Church is important and should be treated as such. But often you have expended so much energy on all the other important matters of life that when you finally get around to church, you feel exhausted and unmotivated. This makes you feel guilty and even condemned for not being more excited about serving the Lord in a practical way at church. But it isn't really a question of desire; it's a question of energy. Already your body and mind have almost been pushed to the brink!

Then there are family responsibilities. If you have an elderly person in your family, you know that this requires attention and energy too. Of course, you want to do this! This isn't an obligation; it is a privilege to take care of older family members. Nevertheless, it still takes time and energy. And if you live in an area where you are close to cousins, aunts, uncles, brothers, sisters, and grandparents, you must also work all these precious people into the schedule. Birthdays, anniversaries, funerals, and weddings — all of these are part of your family responsibilities that require your time, energy, and finances.

How about your friendship responsibilities? Friendships require time and attention. As a good friend, you want to be there for your friend's good times and bad times. You probably believe that you should be available when they need to talk about a problem. You want to spend time with your friends because you need and enjoy their fellowship. But all this requires time and energy as well.

Don't forget your financial challenges and pressures. Life is expensive. Car insurance, life insurance, house payments, credit card payments, groceries, electricity and air-conditioning bills, expenses for the kids to play sports or go to summer camp, clothes for growing children, repairs on the car — and on and on it goes. Plus, you must be faithful in paying your tithes to your church, and you want to give special offerings to other ministries too.

One of Satan's greatest weapons is discouragement, and he knows exactly when to use it. He waits until you are tired, weak, and susceptible to his lies. Then he hits you hard in your emotions, trying to tell you that you are accomplishing nothing valuable in life.

In those moments when I feel physically exhausted and yet I see no pause in my schedule, I turn to Romans 8:11 for encouragement. It says, "But if the Spirit of him that raised up Jesus from the dead dwell in you, he that raised up Christ from the dead shall also quicken your mortal bodies by his Spirit that dwelleth in you."

I especially focus on the phrase that says, "...he that raised up Christ from the dead shall also quicken your mortal bodies...." Our mortal bodies simply have limitations, and there is nothing we can do about it. These limitations are one of the reasons we become physically tired. But in those moments when we need extra strength to keep going, this verse promises that the Holy Spirit will "quicken" our mortal bodies.

The word "quicken" is the Greek word *zoopoieo*, from the word *zoe* and *poieo*. The word *zoe* is the Greek word for life, and it often describes the life of God. The word *poieo* means to do. When these two words are compounded, it means to make alive with life. It carries the idea of to revitalize; to rejuvenate; or to refresh with new life!

This means that if you will yield to the Holy Spirit who dwells in you, He will supernaturally revitalize you. He will rejuvenate you. He will refresh you with a brand-new surge of supernatural life. He will fill you with so much resurrection power that you will be ready to get up and go again!

My Prayer for Today

Lord, I admit that I need a fresh surge of supernatural power in my life right now. I ask You to release the resurrection power of Jesus Christ that resides in my spirit. Let it flow up into my body and mind so I can be rejuvenated and recharged with enough power to fulfill all the responsibilities and duties that lie before me. I know that in my own strength, I can't do everything that is required of me in the days ahead. But I also know that with Your supernatural power working in me, I will be able to do everything You have asked me to do!

I pray this in Jesus' name!

My Confession for Today

I confess that God's Spirit is quickening my mortal flesh and rejuvenating me with enough strength to fulfill all the duties and responsibilities that lie ahead of me. I am not weak. I am not tired. I am refreshed. I am strengthened. I am filled with power. Because the Holy Spirit dwells in me, there is not a single moment when I don't have everything that I need!

I declare this by faith in Jesus' name!

Questions for You to Consider

1. Have you been feeling a little depleted lately? If so, have you asked the Holy Spirit to release resurrection power in you so that you can be supernaturally rejuvenated?

_____

_____

_____

_____

_____

_____

2. Can you think of one particular time when you were physically exhausted, but in one instant you were so filled with life and power that your weakness left, and you were magnificently empowered?

_____

_____

_____

_____

_____

_____

3. Instead of shutting this book and running to your next thing to do, why don't you take a few minutes and ask the Holy Spirit to fill you with power right now?

_____

_____

_____

_____

_____

_____

Day 24

God's Delivering Power Is Yours!

> *For we would not, brethren, have you ignorant of our trouble which came to us in Asia, that we were pressed out of measure, above strength, insomuch that we despaired even of life: But we had the sentence of death in ourselves, that we should not trust in ourselves, but in God which raiseth the dead.*
>
> **— 2 Corinthians 1:8,9**

Everyone has had to endure hardness at some point in life, including the apostle Paul. He describes some of the hardships he endured in Asia in Second Corinthians 1:8,9: "For we would not, brethren, have you ignorant of our trouble which came to us in Asia, that we were pressed out of measure, above strength, insomuch that we despaired even of life: But we had the sentence of death in ourselves, that we should not trust in ourselves, but in God which raiseth the dead."

Notice the first part of verse 8, where Paul says, "For we would not, brethren, have you ignorant of the trouble which came unto us in Asia...." The word "trouble" is the Greek word *thlipsis*, which was used to convey the idea of a heavy-pressure situation. In fact, at one point this word was used to depict a victim who was first tied up with rope and laid on his back; then a huge, heavy boulder was slowly lowered upon him until he was crushed! This, indeed, would be a very heavy situation for the man underneath the boulder! He would be in a tight place, under a heavy burden, or in a great squeeze.

By using this word, Paul is saying, "We were under a heavy load — an unbelievably heavy amount of stress and pressure! We were in very tight circumstances. Our minds were being 'squeezed.' It felt like our lives were being pushed right out of us!"

You might think Paul is referring to physical suffering. Of course, physical suffering is difficult, but the greatest suffering of all always occurs in the mind — mental suffering. A person can live with pain in his body if his mind is still in control. However, when the suffering begins to work on that person's mind, both his body and his mind could eventually break and fold.

Paul's greatest suffering was not physical, but mental. This is why he goes on to say, "...that we were pressed out of measure, above strength, insomuch that we despaired even of life" (v. 8). Particularly pay heed to that first phrase, "that we were pressed out of measure." This is the Greek phrase *kath huperbole*, and it is extremely important in Paul's testimony. It literally means to throw beyond, to excel, to exceed, or to go beyond anything normal or expected. It also describes something that is excessive and beyond the normal range of what most would experience.

By using this word, Paul says, "We were under an amount of pressure that is not normal. It was FAR BEYOND anything we had ever previously experienced.

It was excessive, unbelievable, unbearable, and far too much for any one human being to endure."

Paul goes on to tell us that this pressure was "above strength." This word "above" is also important. It is the Greek word *huper*, which always conveys the idea of something excessive. In order to explain how bad his situation was, Paul is piling words on top of words, all of which accurately portray how terrifically bad the ordeal in Asia was for him and his traveling companions.

It is almost as though Paul is saying, "Normal human strength never would have been sufficient for this situation. The strength it required was far, far beyond human strength. This predicament required strength in a measure I had never previously needed. It was beyond me!"

Then Paul says, "...insomuch that we despaired even of life...." The Greek word for "despaired" is the word *exaporeomai*. It was used in a technical sense to describe no way out. It is where we get our word exasperated, and it describes people who feel trapped, caught, up against the wall, pinned down, and utterly hopeless. Today we might say, "Sorry, but it looks like this is the end of the road for you!"

Then Paul continues in verse 9, "But we had the sentence of death in ourselves...." The word "sentence" is the Greek word *apokrima*, which in this sense speaks of a final verdict. Paul is saying, "It looked to us like the verdict was in, and we were not going to survive."

When all these different phrases and words are looked at together, it becomes very plain that Paul's primary suffering at this moment was mental, not physical. He is describing mental agony on a measure that few of us have ever experienced.

Because of all these Greek words, the following could be taken as an interpretive translation of these verses:

"We would not, brethren, have you ignorant of the horribly tight, life-threatening squeeze that came to us in Asia. It was unbelievable! With all the things that we have been through, this was the worst of all. It felt like our lives were being crushed! It was so difficult that I didn't know what to do. No experience I've ever been through required so much of me; in fact, I didn't have enough strength to cope with it. Toward the end of this ordeal, I was so overwhelmed that I didn't think we'd ever get out! I felt suffocated, trapped, and pinned against the wall. I really thought it was the end of the road for us! As far as we were concerned, the verdict was in, and the verdict said, 'Death.' But really, this was no great shock, because we were already feeling the effect of death and depression in our souls...."

Paul doesn't tell us exactly what happened to him and his team when they were in Asia. But whatever it was, it was the most grueling experience they had ever been through until that time.

You may ask, "Why would Paul want us to know that he had been through such difficult times? Did he want us to feel sorry for him?" Absolutely not! Paul wanted us to know that everyone endures hardness from time to time. Even the greatest, most well-known, celebrated spiritual leaders are confronted with situations that are devastating or challenging.

You see, even with all his knowledge, revelation, and experience, Paul was still assaulted by the devil. That assault was so aggressive that Paul wrote "we despaired even of life," describing the intense emotions he felt as he went through these extremely difficult circumstances.

But Paul didn't break, and he didn't die! Likewise, if you'll hold on and fight right where you are, you also won't break or be destroyed! Like Paul, you will win the victory. Then you'll be able to say that the ordeal happened in order that you would not trust in yourself, "...but in God which raiseth the dead: Who delivered us from so great a death, and doth deliver..." (2 Corinthians 1:9,10).

God's delivering power is yours! He has rescued you in the past; He will rescue you now; and He will rescue you again and again in the future. All He asks is that you "stay put" right where He called you — refusing to move, rejecting every temptation to give up, and deciding never to give in to the pressure that the devil wants to pile on top of you. If you'll be faithful and slug it out with the power and armor of God, you'll discover that God will be with you all the way through to a successful conclusion!

My Prayer for Today

Lord, You have never abandoned me, and You never will! When the devil tries to crush me with stress, I throw the weight of my cares upon You. I can't thank You enough for taking all those pressures off my shoulders and freeing me to walk in peace! My heart is simply overflowing with gratefulness for the strength and power You have released inside me. I know that with Your continued help, I shall be victorious, and these problems will flee!

I pray this in Jesus' name!

My Confession for Today

I confess that God's delivering power is mine! He has rescued me before; He will rescue me now; and He will rescue me when I need His power again in the future. I am "staying put" right where God called me. I refuse to move; I reject every temptation to give up; and I will never give in to the pressures to stop doing what God has told me to do. I will be faithful, and God will empower me to make it all the way through to my place of victory!

I declare this by faith in Jesus' name!

Questions for You to Consider

1. Can you think of a time when you underwent circumstances so difficult that you wondered if you would survive the situation? You obviously survived, so what was the one thing that most helped you get through that ordeal?

----

2. As you think of others who are going through hard times right now, what is the most effective thing you could do to help them get past their difficult circumstances?

----

3. Why don't you make a list of ten practical things you can do to encourage these people and to remind them that you are standing with them in faith until they come through this ordeal in victory?

_____

_____

_____

_____

_____

_____

Day 25

Have You Paid Attention to Yourself Lately?

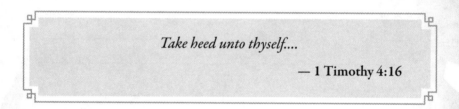

Take heed unto thyself....

— 1 Timothy 4:16

Are you constantly serving others without giving yourself needed times of rest and refreshing? Or do you remember that you have spiritual needs too?

When Paul wrote First Timothy 4:16, Timothy was a young pastor working ferociously to see his ministry succeed. Timothy was serving as the pastor of the giant church of Ephesus — the world's largest church at that time. In the process, he was learning to deal with all the problems that go along with serving as the senior pastor of such a large church.

Timothy was discovering that taking care of a large church was an all-consuming task. He was giving every ounce of himself to serve the needs of that church and to make sure it was well taken care of. In fact, he was so busy taking care of everything and everyone else that he was forgetting to take care of himself!

Have you ever been guilty of running around and taking care of everyone else except yourself? Have you ever gotten so busy helping others that you forfeited your own vital time with God? Be honest! Have you ever done this so regularly that you began to feel drained, and you knew it was because you weren't taking care of your own spiritual needs?

That's why Paul admonished Timothy, "Take heed unto thyself...." This phrase "take heed" comes from the Greek word *epecho*, which is a compound of the words *ep* and *echo*. The word *ep* means on, and the word *echo* means to have or to hold. When these two words are compounded into one word, it means to grab hold of something very tightly. In other words, the word *epecho* describes an extremely firm grip.

It's so easy to get distracted by other things that scream for your attention. However, if your relationship with God suffers because you are trying to help everyone else, it will just be a matter of time until you run dry, lose your energy and passion, and have nothing more to offer. This is exactly what was happening to Timothy! If he was to continue serving as an effective minister to other people, he had to set aside some private time to develop his own relationship with God.

Paul's words to Timothy could be translated:

"Get ahold of yourself...." "Make your own spiritual life a priority...." "Don't get so busy that you forget you have spiritual needs too...."

It's good to serve the Lord and to be willing to work. You should be faithful to whatever He has called you to do. But you should never get so busy that you forget your own spiritual needs and thus end up running dry of spiritual power. Take Paul's words to heart. Never forget to "take heed unto thyself"!

If you are going to serve God and do His will for years to come, it is essential that you make your own spiritual life your first priority. After all, you can give only what you have inside you. If you run dry because you never spend time with the Lord, it won't be long until you have nothing left to give to anyone!

So, if you wish to continue being effective for God's Kingdom, it is mandatory that you don't forget about your own spiritual need to grow and to be refreshed by the Word. As Paul's words could be understood, "Don't get so busy that you forget you have spiritual needs too!"

My Prayer for Today

Lord, help me remember not to neglect my own spiritual life. My time with You is vital if I am to remain spiritually fresh and empowered to serve others. When life gets so busy that I think there is no time to spend with You, help me refocus and reschedule my life so that my relationship with You remains my greatest priority. And after I've been refreshed by Your Word and Your Presence, help me then to minister the fullness of Your Spirit and Your love to those around me.

I pray this in Jesus' name!

My Confession for Today

I boldly proclaim by faith that my spiritual life is my number-one priority. I pay attention to my walk with God, and I do everything I can do to make sure my spiritual life is alive, growing, and constantly reaching out for more of the Lord. I am sensitive to God's Spirit. I am attuned to His Word. As a result of putting my own spiritual life first, I am filled with enough power and love to adequately serve the needs of those who are around me.

I declare this by faith in Jesus' name!

Questions for You to Consider

1. How much time do you personally spend alone with God every day?

   _____

   _____

   _____

   _____

   _____

   _____

2. Have you gotten so busy serving the Lord that you have neglected your own walk with Him? If so, write down any problems you may be facing in different areas of your life because of this neglect.

   _____

   _____

   _____

   _____

   _____

   _____

3. What steps do you need to take to reverse this situation and refocus on your relationship with Jesus?

_____

_____

_____

_____

_____

_____

Day 26

You Are Never Alone!

> *Wherefore seeing we also are compassed about with so great a cloud of witnesses....*
>
> — **Hebrews 12:1**

At times you may have wondered, *Has anyone else ever experienced the kinds of problems I'm experiencing right now, or am I out here all alone?*

No, you're not alone! Hebrews 11 records the remarkable feats of faith accomplished by various people in the Old Testament. These were people who had to fight and struggle as they waited for the object of their faith to manifest. Their walk of faith was a great, great challenge.

Because these Old Testament saints stayed with what God had told them to do and never gave up, they eventually saw His blessings begin to operate in their lives. Nevertheless, nearly all of them endured great, difficult hardships and challenges before their victory came.

To let us know that we're not alone in our own walk of faith, the writer of Hebrews says, "Wherefore seeing we also are compassed about with so great a cloud of witnesses, let us lay aside every weight, and the sin which doth so easily beset us, and let us run with patience the race that is set before us" (Hebrews 12:1).

Notice that it says, "Wherefore seeing we also are compassed about with so great a cloud of witnesses...." The phrase "compassed about" is taken from the word *peikeimenai*, which is a compound of the words *peri* and *keimai*. The word *peri* means around or to be completely encircled by something. The second part of the word, *keimai*, means to lie down. When these two words are compounded into one word, they mean to lie around, as if something has been piled high and is lying all around you on every side. This is the portrayal of being completely encircled by something that is stacked high on every side!

Therefore, this verse carries the following idea:

> *"Wherefore seeing we have lying all around us on every side...."*
> *"Wherefore seeing these biblical examples are piled up and lying all around us...."*

The Bible is piled high with examples of people — people just like you — who stood in faith and endured difficulties in order to do the will of God. You are surrounded on every side with powerful examples of people who were challenged in their faith, yet who held fast to the Word of God. And as a result, these godly people saw God's promises come to pass in their lives!

You are not alone!

❧ Look at Noah and the fight he endured.

❧ Look at Abraham and the fight he endured.

- Look at Sarah and the fight she endured.

- Look at Jacob and the fight he endured.

- Look at Joseph and the fight he endured.

- Look at Moses and the fight he endured.

- Look at Gideon, Barak, Samson, Jephthah, David, Samuel, and the prophets and the fight they all endured.

Take some time today to read some of these examples from the Old Testament — and then turn to the New Testament to see the many examples of faithful people who are also listed there. The Bible is packed full of examples of those who heard from God, who took His Word deep into their hearts, and who refused to stop until they saw the fulfillment of what God had promised them. Like you, they faced hardships and challenges. But no matter what obstacles stood in their way, they kept going and never stopped until God's plan for their lives was accomplished.

According to Hebrews 12:1, there are so many people who fit this description that they are literally all around you. Don't think you can only look to the Bible for these godly examples. If you look closely, you'll see that there are huge numbers of these "never-give-up" kind of people living on this earth right now as well. You are not alone in your walk of faith!

Don't let the devil tell you that you're the only one who has faced this kind of circumstance, because many have gone before you who have faced the same battles and won great victories. If you'll commit a few minutes of your time to read Hebrews 11, I believe you'll find that your battle isn't worse than the battles these saints fought and won. Reading these verses will encourage your heart!

Don't give up and throw in the towel! Hard times will pass, and you will see the Word of God bring you the victory you desire. When you're tempted to get discouraged, just remember the many examples piled up all around you of people who endured and later won their prize!

My Prayer for Today

Lord, Your Word says nothing is impossible to those who believe, so I am releasing my faith in Your promises. I fully believe that what You did for those faithful believers, You will also do for me!

I pray this in Jesus' name!

My Confession for Today

I confess that I have victory over the challenges I face in life! I know that many have faced the same battles I'm facing and victoriously won their fight. My battle isn't worse than the battles others have faced, so I boldly declare that I will be triumphant in my fight, just as they were triumphant in theirs! It is a fact that hard times will pass — and when they do, I will see the Word of God bring me the victory that I declare and desire! It is not a matter of IF I will win, but only a question of WHEN I will win!

 I declare this by faith in Jesus' name!

Questions for You to Consider

1. What are some of your past victories that you can encourage yourself with as you fight your current fight of faith?

    _____

    _____

    _____

    _____

    _____

    _____

2. In each of those past struggles, what helped you to stay in the fight until you won?

    _____

    _____

    _____

    _____

    _____

    _____

3. List some examples of people in your life and in the Bible who held fast to God's promises as they faced great difficulties until their victory was finally won.

_____

_____

_____

_____

_____

_____

Day 27

Do Whatever Is Necessary to Keep Envy and Strife Out of Your Life!

> *For where envying and strife is, there is confusion and every evil work.*
>
> **— James 3:16**

The devil knows that envy and strife destroy relationships and long-term friendships. He is aware that if he can create envy and strife between you and the ones you love, he can ruin those special relationships that God intended to be a blessing in your life. Do you have any relationships in your life right now that are under this kind of demonic assault?

The devil doesn't just target friendships with this type of assault. He also knows how to get in between you and your church family, a ministry you love and support, or even the organization or place of business where you work. The enemy doesn't care whom he divides — he simply wants to divide! Since envy and strife are some of the tools he uses to do this, it is crucial that you understand how to recognize envy and strife and how to stand against them!

In James 3:16, the Bible says, "For where envying and strife is, there is confusion and every evil work." I want you to notice the word "envy" in this verse. It is taken from the Greek word *zelos*, and it denotes a fierce desire to promote one's own ideas and convictions to the exclusion of everyone else. This word *zelos* is where we get the word zealot, which describes a person who is so fixated, obsessed, and fanatical about his own cause that others perceive him as an extremist on the threshold of becoming militant.

In the case of James 3:16, this word presents a picture of a believer who is so obsessed, gripped, and preoccupied with his own view of things that he can't see or hear the view of anyone else. In fact, his militant perspective has made him lopsided in his thinking. He never takes a softer line but holds out until all the other parties admit defeat and agree with his point of view.

Therefore, the word "envy" in James 3:16 could be translated this way:

> *"For where there is a fierce desire to promote one's own ideas and convictions to the elimination of everyone else...."*

If this kind of attitude continues, it will naturally lead to the next step in this horrible sequence of events. This is where strife comes into the picture! Notice that James goes on to say, "For where envying and strife is...."

The word "strife" is taken from the Greek word *eritheia*. It was used by the ancient Greeks to stand for a political party. This Greek word is often translated as a party spirit because of its linkage to political systems and political parties. Therefore, in order for us to understand why James used this word, we need to stop and think about the way political parties are formed and how they function.

Political parties are formed by a group of people who have similar values and views. After the party is formed, the participants develop a unified agenda; once the agenda is decided on, they create a platform. From that platform, the people begin to push their agenda and ideas, fighting fiercely to see that their party's platform is accepted and eventually put in the position of ruling and calling the shots.

In the same way, some Christians become so clouded by their ambition to see their own views adopted that they have no tolerance for anyone who sees things differently than they do. These people usually gravitate to other believers who hold similar views.

Once these "like-minded" Christians find each other, they naturally begin to take sides, forming a kind of allegiance. Then they begin to form agendas and develop plans to see their views pushed, promoted, and accepted. As a result, people who once stood shoulder to shoulder often end up standing on different sides of a fight with their relationships ruined and filled with hurt.

When envy and strife have made it this far, the next step in this sequence of events becomes inevitable. James 3:16 continues, "For where envying and strife is, there is confusion...."

The word "confusion" is taken from the word *akatastasia*. It was used in New Testament times to describe civil disobedience, disorder, and anarchy in a city, state, or government. By using this word, James explicitly tells us that when situations of strife and discord are allowed to persist, an atmosphere of anarchy sets in and begins to destroy the relationships once loved and cherished. Rational thinking is replaced by raw emotions, and people end up getting hurt.

James wants to make sure we understand what this kind of conduct eventually produces if this behavior isn't stopped. He goes on to say, "For where envying and strife is, there is confusion and every evil work."

The word "evil" is from the word *phaulos*, describing something that is terribly bad or exceedingly vile. We get the word "foul" from this Greek word. James is saying that where envy and strife are permitted to operate, thus producing confusion and anarchy in relationships, they ultimately yield a foul-smelling situation!

These various Greek words in James 3:16 convey this idea:

> *"For where there is a fierce desire to promote one's own ideas and convictions to the exclusion of everyone else's, it produces divisions so great that people end up taking sides and forming differing parties with conflicting agendas. This is a terrible event, because it creates great unrest among people who should be united. Ultimately, the whole situation becomes a stinking mess!"*

But understand this: You can help stop this from happening by choosing to consider other people's opinions to be just as important as your own! Instead of pushing your own agenda, why not stop and listen to what others have to say? They may have something powerful to contribute, but if you can't hear them, you'll never benefit from their perspective.

You don't have to yield to envy and strife! When the opportunity for strife arises, you can beat Satan at his own game by choosing to make room for the ideas, thoughts, and opinions of others. Even if you don't agree with what they say, at least you can demonstrate that you value their right to have a differing opinion. By maintaining an attitude of staying on the same side as your fellow believers, you can put the devil on the run and keep your relationships alive, healthy, and long-lasting!

My Prayer for Today

Lord, I ask You to forgive me for the times I have allowed strife to get into my heart. Also, please forgive me for those occasions when I have been the origin of strife and fighting. Help me grow in discernment so I can quickly recognize when the devil is trying to create division. Show me how to be a peacekeeper and a source of harmony rather than a player in the midst of others' wrong attitudes.

I pray this in Jesus' name!

My Confession for Today

I confess that I do not yield to envy and strife! When the opportunity for strife arises, I beat Satan at his own game by choosing to respectfully make room for the ideas, thoughts, and opinions of others. Even if I don't agree with what they say, I let them know that I value their right to have a differing opinion. I maintain an attitude of staying on the same side with my fellow believers; therefore, I put the devil on the run and keep him OUT of my relationships!

I declare this by faith in Jesus' name!

Questions for You to Consider

1. Do your coworkers, friends, and family members find you open-hearted to their suggestions, or do they find it difficult to express themselves honestly in front of you?

    _____

    _____

    _____

    _____

    _____

    _____

2. When the opportunity for strife arises, what can you do to circumvent it and promote peace?

    _____

    _____

    _____

    _____

    _____

3. Can you recall moments when you were so sure you were right, only to discover that someone else's idea was really much better than yours?

_____

_____

_____

_____

_____

_____

Day 28

It's Time for You to Lay Aside Every Unnecessary Weight

> *Wherefore seeing we are compassed about with so great a cloud of witnesses, let us lay aside every weight....*
>
> — **Hebrews 12:1**

What is it that keeps hindering you from living a life of obedience? Do you struggle with a particular sin, habit, attitude, or fear that keeps you from running your race of faith the way you ought? If so, you probably already know what it is, and I'd guess that you've already prayed, prayed, and prayed for victory in overcoming that problem because you really do want to please God.

Every now and then, we all tolerate things in our lives that make it difficult for us to please God. And when we know we're not pleasing God, we typically aren't happy with ourselves either. This is one reason that Hebrews 12:1 tells us to "...lay aside every weight...."

The words "lay aside" are taken from the Greek word *apotithimi*, a compound of the words *apo* and *tithimi*. The word *apo* means away, and the word *tithimi* means to place or to lay something down. When these two words are compounded together, it gives a picture of someone who is laying something down while at the same time he is pushing it far away from himself. It means to lay something down and to push it far away and beyond reach. Thus, this word implies a deliberate decision to make a permanent change of attitude and behavior.

Removing wrong attitudes and actions from our lives will not occur accidentally. We must decide to change — to remove, to lay aside, and to put away attitudes and actions that don't please God and adversely affect our walk of faith.

Hebrews 12:1 refers to these incorrect attitudes and actions as "weights." The word "weight" is from the Greek word *ogkos* — a word that describes a burden or something so heavy and cumbersome that it impedes a runner from running his race as he should.

This word was particularly used in the athletic world to signify the actions of an athlete who would deliberately strip himself of excess weight before participating in a competition. This stripping process included the loss of excess flesh through dieting and exercise. Then on the day of the actual competition, he stripped off nearly all his clothes so no extra weight would slow him down. He had his eye on the prize, so he was determined to strip off all "weight" that might potentially keep him from being the best athlete he could be.

This sends a strong message to us! If we want to please God, satisfy ourselves, and do something significant with our lives, we have to choose to remove anything from our lives that would hinder those objectives.

The athlete of the ancient world didn't become "unweighted" by accident. He dropped all excess weight on purpose. He dieted; he exercised; and he shed every other unnecessary weight he could find to shed. This stripping process demanded his attention, his decision, and his devotion. It wasn't going to happen by accident, so he had to initiate the process of removal.

What if those athletes had tried to run their race with loads of extra weight? They certainly wouldn't have been able to run very far! This is exactly what sinful habits and attitudes do to your walk with the Lord. If you don't remove them, they will eventually weigh you down and knock you out of your race of faith!

The Holy Spirit is urging you and me to take a good look at our lives and then remove everything that weighs us down and keeps us from a life of obedience. We must be honest with ourselves and with God.

Do you have a habit or a wrong attitude that binds you? Are you plagued by a fear that weighs you down and keeps you from fulfilling your potential in Christ? Make a rock-solid, quality decision today to grab hold of those unnecessary burdens and remove, lay aside, and permanently put them away from your life.

Once you make that decision, you'll find yourself running your race of faith with much more ease as you press on to victory!

My Prayer for Today

Lord, I know that You're on my side and that You want to help me. So today I'm asking You to help me lay aside the attitudes, negative thought patterns, and bad habits that keep pulling me back down into miserable defeat. I'm exhausted from trying to live for You while dragging along these old weights behind me at the same time. I need to drop them and leave them behind! So today I am asking You to help me make the big break. Help me make this the day I permanently drop all the unnecessary weights that hinder me and walk away from them forever!

I pray this in Jesus' name!

My Confession for Today

I confess that I live a life of obedience! Sin, bad habits, negative attitudes, and fear have no influence in my life. Because I am free of these things, I am able to run my race of faith without any hindrances caused by my own actions. Because I want to please God, I do not tolerate things in my life that make it difficult for me to walk by faith or to please God. Absolutely nothing is more important to me than knowing God's will and doing it in a way that brings pleasure to the Lord!

I declare this by faith in Jesus' name!

Questions for You to Consider

1. What is the first thing that comes to mind when you think of a "weight" that has been keeping you from running your race with grace and ease lately?

    _____

    _____

    _____

    _____

    _____

    _____

2. How can you strip yourself today of that "weight" so you can stay in the race to win God's prize for your life?

    _____

    _____

    _____

    _____

    _____

    _____

3. Write down three ways you can please God, satisfy yourself, and do something significant in your life this week.

_____

_____

_____

_____

_____

_____

Day 29

Keep the Devil Where He Belongs— Under Your Feet!

> *And the God of peace shall bruise Satan under your feet shortly....*
>
> — **Romans 16:20**

Are you tired of the devil blocking your way and causing all kinds of disruptions and problems in your life, such as problems in your relationships, financial woes, or health problems? How would you like to lift your foot high and then slam it down as hard as you can on top of the devil — pounding, hammering, trouncing, crushing, and smattering him to bits under your feet? Does that sound like something you wish you could do?

Believe it or not, the apostle Paul encourages you to do exactly that! In Romans 16:20 he writes, "And the God of peace shall bruise Satan under your feet shortly...." The word "bruise" is taken from the Greek word *suntribo*, a word that significantly presents this notion of trampling the devil under your feet. The word was historically used to denote the act of smashing grapes into wine. However, it was also used to refer to the act of snapping, breaking, and crushing bones. In fact, it pictures bones that have been utterly crushed beyond recognition.

This word *suntribo* is used in Mark 5:4, where the Bible tells us about the demon-possessed man of the Gadarenes. It says, "Because that he had been often bound with fetters and chains, and the chains had been plucked asunder by him, and the fetters broken in pieces...." The phrase "broken in pieces" is this same word *suntribo*. Although bound in chains and fetters, the demonized man was sufficiently energized by the demons to be able to crush those fetters to pieces.

The use of the word *suntribo* in this verse portrays a demon-possessed man releasing so much rage and violence that he was able to obliterate, smash, demolish, and reduce those fetters to nothing. When he was finished, the fetters fell to the ground in a heap, twisted and deformed — so broken that they would never be used to hold anyone captive again.

Now Paul uses this same word in Romans 16:20 when he says we are to "bruise" Satan under our feet. However, notice that Paul says we are to bruise him under our feet "shortly." This word "shortly" is extremely important because it takes the whole picture to the next level. It tells us what attitude we must demonstrate the next time the devil tries to get in our way or block our path.

The word "shortly" comes from a military term that described the way Roman soldiers marched in formation. They were instructed by their commanders, "You are Roman soldiers! Lift your feet high, stomp loudly, and let everyone know you are coming through town. The sound of the stomping and pounding of your feet is the signal to let everyone know they need to get out of your way. And if someone is foolish enough to stand in your way — even if someone falls down in front of you — don't you dare stop to ask them to move! Just keep marching, stomping, and pounding, even if it means you have to walk right over them!"

So when Paul uses the word "shortly," he is referring to the pounding, stomping, and crushing steps of a Roman soldier. And remember, Roman soldiers wore shoes that were spiked with nails on the bottom. When a challenger stood in front of them — or if a person fell in their path — these soldiers would simply ignore the obstacle and keep marching, stomping, and pounding along their way, leaving the challenger or unfortunate person completely obliterated and trampled beyond recognition — an ugly, bloody sight.

What does all this mean for you and me today? It means the next time the devil tries to get in your way or block your path, you shouldn't stop to politely ask him to move. If the enemy is stupid enough to challenge you and tries to hinder your plans, God tells you what to do in this verse: "Just keep walking! If the devil tries to stop you, just raise your feet high, pound down as hard as you can, and stomp all over him as you march forward. Crush and bruise him beyond recognition!"

However, it is important to point out that this smashing and crushing of Satan must be done in cooperation with God. Alone you are no match for this archenemy. That's the reason Paul says, "...The God of peace shall bruise Satan under your feet...." In other words, this is a joint partnership between you and God. By yourself, you could never keep Satan subdued. But with God as your Partner, the devil has no chance of ever slipping out from under your heel!

Romans 16:20 suggests this idea:

"The God of peace will smash and completely obliterate Satan under your feet! If Satan tries to get in your way or block your path, then it's time for you to act like a soldier — lift your feet high, stomp and pound down hard, crushing the enemy under your feet and leaving him in a heap, trampled beyond recognition, as you march on...."

The glorious truth is that Jesus already completely destroyed Satan's power over you through His death and resurrection. The devil was utterly smashed, crushed, and bruised when Jesus was victoriously raised from the dead. Your God-given mission now is to reinforce the victory already won and to demonstrate just how miserably defeated Satan already is!

The enemy may try to lord himself over you; he may attempt to exert his foul influence over your life. However, he is merely using empty threats and illusions to feed fear into your mind.

Never forget — the only place that rightfully belongs to the devil is the small space of ground right under your feet! Jesus accomplished a total, complete, and perfect work through the Cross of Calvary and His resurrection from the dead. That means your healing, your miracle, or your financial blessing already belongs to you! The victory is already yours!

My Prayer for Today

Lord, the next time the devil tries to get in my way or to block my path, help me to raise my feet high, pound down as hard as I can, and stomp all over him as I march forward unhindered to do Your will. I thank You that because of Your victory, Satan has no right to exercise this kind of control over my life anymore! With You working as my Partner, I can stare that old enemy in the face and command him to move. And if he tries to put up a fight, I can push him out of the way and walk on through!

I pray this in Jesus' name!

My Confession for Today

I boldly declare that Jesus destroyed Satan's power over me! Through Jesus' death and resurrection, the devil was utterly smashed, crushed, and bruised. Now my God-given mission is to reinforce that glorious victory and to demonstrate just how miserably defeated Satan already is. The enemy may try to lord himself over me, but he has no authority to exercise any control in my life!

I declare this by faith in Jesus' name!

Questions for You to Consider

1. Do you see yourself as a victorious soldier in the army of God?

_____

_____

_____

_____

_____

2. Are your problems under your feet today, or do you feel like you are constantly under the heel of your problems?

_____

_____

_____

_____

_____

3. What are you going to do to turn this situation around? Write down ideas about what actions you can take to start winning the victory over the devil's attacks in your life.

_____

_____

_____

_____

_____

_____

Day 30

You Are What You Are by the Grace of God!

> *But by the grace of God I am what I am....*
>
> — **1 Corinthians 15:10**

When I was young, my father tried to encourage me to join in all kinds of sports along with the other young boys from church and school. He tried to motivate me to get interested in baseball, football, basketball, and even bowling. But there was a problem: I had absolutely no interest in any type of sport that had to do with any kind of a ball. It was all boring and monotonous to me. I gave it my best, but I just didn't have it "in me" to get involved in sports. My heart and my interest were simply not there.

God had made me to enjoy other things, like attending the orchestra, visiting museums, listening to classical music, and taking art lessons to develop my natural artistic talent. But those were not the kinds of things that young boys were "supposed" to be interested in, so I ardently pushed forward — trying to force myself to be interested in sports. But it was to no avail, because I just didn't have an interest in it.

The devil tormented me for years, telling me that there was something wrong with me because I was not like other boys and men who rapturously talked about and played sports. To be honest, sports disgusted me — and decades later, I still have no interest in sports, and I didn't produce any interest in my sons in sports. Even today, we are a "no sports" family. However, we love operas, classical music, art auctions, and other things of that nature. Each one of us is tuned into the world of the arts.

When I was a boy, I thought I was weird because of how I was made. But now that I live in Russia, where classical art, music, ballet, and arts of all sorts are a vital part of the culture, I understand that God created me exactly the way I needed to be for my assignment in the former USSR. Furthermore, He designed our sons' desires to align with this culture. In Russia, we are perfectly fitted for the world around us. God knew all of that when I was a young boy. At the time, I struggled with coming to terms with my disinterest in sports and the reason why I had such a profoundly deep love for the arts. But it was all a part of how God needed me to be "fitted" for where I would live the bulk of my adult life.

The truth is, many people secretly struggle with why they are the way they are. Some are deeply affected by their characteristics that others might perceive as shortcomings, whereas others have learned to overlook them. For some, the devil has used these feelings as a launching pad to tell them there is something wrong with them — and he has convinced many that they are indeed an aberration from what other people are like.

But I want to tell you that God fashioned you perfectly for His calling and gifting in your life. Your "fitting" may be different from what is considered normal in your neighborhood, but that does not mean something is wrong with you. It just means God has "fitted" you for something that your neighbors will probably never do! Let them enjoy who they are, and you need to learn to accept yourself and enjoy who God made you to be!

I don't know anyone else from my hometown who has a ministry in the heart of Moscow, Russia. The vast majority of people I grew up with and attended school with are living the American dream. But God knew that would not be my life, so He designed me for my own unique calling.

Thankfully, I had a mother who understood there was something different about me and encouraged me to pursue my interests. My father never understood when I was young, but as I grew older and the call of God on my life became more evident, he came to understand why I never fit the mold of other boys in our church and school. It took time for him to grasp it, but before he went to Heaven, my dad fully understood and encouraged me in who I am. Amen!

Have you ever felt like a misfit? If so, let me encourage you with a verse that I've spoken to myself over and over through the years. Especially in years when I struggled with my differences from others, I learned to lean on the truth of this verse. It is First Corinthians 15:10, where Paul says, "But by the grace of God I am what I am…."

When Paul wrote this verse, he was writing about how different he was from all the other apostles. They had walked with Jesus; he had not. His knowledge of Christ came from direct revelation, whereas the other apostles had walked with Jesus, heard His voice, felt His tender touch, and witnessed His earthly ministry. Paul, however, had been called into apostolic ministry by revelation, and this put him in a category that made him different from all the other apostles. They could all lay claim to an earthly experience with Christ that Paul could not claim.

Is it possible that Paul was tempted to feel inferior because his experience was different from theirs? I think the answer may be yes, because in First Corinthians 15:8 and 9, he wrote, "And last of all, he was seen of me also, as of one born out of due time. For I am least of the apostles that am not meet to be called an apostle...." Yet he was one of the mightiest apostles; he wrote more of the New Testament than anyone else; and he traveled to more of the Gentile world than any other apostle of that time. His education, his travels, his love of languages — it all perfectly outfitted Paul for the ministry God had entrusted to him.

When Paul wrote, "But by the grace of God I am what I am...," it was his recognition that everything that made him who he was uniquely prepared him to fulfill his purpose by the grace of God. So rather than focus on the fact that he was different from others, Paul continued by saying, "But by the grace of God I am what I am, and his grace which was bestowed upon me was not in vain; but I labored more abundantly than they all: yet not I, but the grace of God which was with me."

According to Paul, God's grace was bestowed on him, and it was not in "vain." The word "vain" is the Greek word *kenos*, and it describes something that is empty, wasted, or void. Paul declared that the grace of God, which poured mightily into his life, did not produce hollow results. Rather, he said, "I labored more abundantly than they all; yet not I, but the grace of God which was with me."

The word "labored" is the Greek word *kopiao*, which describes labor and work of the most intense type. The word "abundantly" comes from a form of the word *perissos*, and it is comparative, which means Paul was essentially saying, "Compared to the other apostles, I worked harder than any of them." But he went on to acknowledge that it was not he alone doing this strenuous, nonstop work; it was the grace of God that was at work within him. The word "grace" here is *charis*, which denotes the empowering presence of God.

Paul was indeed different than the other apostles. But he was mightily anointed and perfectly gifted and fitted for the call God had given him to reach the Gentile world. And although Paul had no earthly experience with Jesus like the other apostles did, he was no less an apostle. On the contrary, he was a mighty, world-changing force for the Gospel. But Paul had to come to a place where he surrendered his inadequate feelings and accepted the fact that he was what he was by the grace of God.

Today I want to tell you to stop badgering yourself if you are a little different from others. You may not have realized it, but if everyone was alike, it would be a pretty uninteresting world to live in. Your differences make you unique. God made you with certain characteristics and personality traits because you need them for the assignment He has planned for your life. So rather than struggle with yourself or put yourself down for being a little different from others, it's time for you to claim First Corinthians 15:10 and declare, "I AM WHAT I AM BY THE GRACE OF GOD!"

My Prayer for Today

Father, I ask You to help me really see and realize that the way You made me is not a mistake. You have fitted me exactly for the call that You have placed upon my life. Although I may be different from others around me, it is OKAY, because my call is different than that of my neighbors and friends. I confess that I've struggled with myself, but today I surrender it all — and I thank You that I am what I am by the grace of God. I ask You to help me understand it and receive it. With the help of Your grace, any self-imposed self-rejection I have lived under comes to an end. I receive Your grace; I accept who You have made me to be; and I confidently shine as a trophy of Your masterful making!

I pray this in Jesus' name!

My Confession for Today

I confess that I am made exactly as God intended for me to be made. He fitted me with thoughts, gifts, and talents that may be different from others, but they are essential for what God has called me to do. These differences will be precisely what is needed when I fully step forward into the plan that God has designed for me and my family. I have battered myself long enough — and starting today, I accept who I am and what the grace of God has made me to be!

I declare this by faith in Jesus' name!

Questions for You to Consider

1. Let's think about it: Haven't there been many people in the Bible who were fashioned differently from their contemporaries, but it was because God had a special call on their lives that required them to be different?

_____

_____

_____

_____

_____

_____

2. Who are some of those Bible characters? Take time to consider those who grew up differently from those around them with different gifts and different dreams because God had a special path for them to take in life.

_____

_____

_____

_____

_____

_____

3. Can you think of individuals outside of the Bible in secular realms who were seen as "different" from the time they were young, yet their differences contributed to their success in life? Who are some of those individuals?

_____

_____

_____

_____

_____

_____

Day 31

The Holy Spirit of Peace
Is Our Comforter

> *And I will pray the Father, and he shall give you another Comforter....*
>
> — John 14:16

As Jesus taught His disciples about the Holy Spirit during their last night together in the Upper Room, He referred to the Holy Spirit as the "Comforter" on four separate occasions (*see* John 14:16, 14:26, 15:26, and John 16:7). For Jesus to repeat this title four times in the space of three chapters tells us that the point He is making must be very important. When a truth is repeated in quick succession in Scripture, it is always for the sake of emphasis.

Here we find that Jesus was trying to penetrate His disciples' hearts — as well as our own hearts — with the truth of the Holy Spirit's role as a "Comforter" so they would fully understand it. However, to fully comprehend the message Jesus was trying to convey, we must look to the original Greek language to understand exactly what the word "Comforter" means.

This title of "Comforter" is actually a translation of the Greek word *parakletos*, which is a compound of two Greek words *para* and *kaleo*. For now, I am going to focus on the first part of this compound word, the word *para*.[1]

Simply put, the word *para* means *alongside*, and it carries the idea of near proximity or being very close to someone or something else. However, this term is quite versatile and can thus be seen in a variety of contexts throughout Scripture. Let's look at several New Testament examples to glean a better sense of its meaning.

The Bible says in Luke 5:1, "And it came to pass, that, as the people pressed upon him to hear the word of God, he stood *by* the lake of Gennesaret." The word "by" in this verse is a translation of the Greek word *para*. Here it conveys Jesus' close proximity to the lake of Gennesaret. He literally stood *alongside* this lake as He preached to the multitudes.

In Mark 5:21, which follows the account of Jesus casting out a legion of demons from the demoniac of the Gadarenes, this term is used in a similar way. Mark records, "And when Jesus was passed over again by ship unto the other side, much people gathered unto him: and he was *nigh unto* the sea." The phrase "nigh unto" is also a translation of the word *para*, and it tells us that so many people were pressing forward to touch Jesus that He couldn't even get away from the water's edge. He was forced to walk *alongside* the sea.

---

[1]   For more on this subject, please see Rick Renner's book *Sparkling Gems From the Greek, Volume 2* (Shippensburg, PA: Harrison House, 2016).

In Second Timothy 2:2, we see a different usage of the word *para*. Here Paul used it to describe his close relationship with Timothy, writing, "And the things that thou hast heard of me among many witnesses, the same commit thou to faithful men, who shall be able to teach others also." When Paul said, "...and the things thou has learned *of* me...," the word "of" is the Greek word *para*. This conveys powerful information regarding Paul and Timothy's relationship to one another. The elderly apostle was reminding Timothy, "You learned everything *para* me. I allowed you come *alongside* me."

As a current example from my own life, I could say that my wife is *para*, or *alongside*, me. She lives with me, talks with me, shops with me, travels with me, prays with me, pastors with me, and has reared our children with me. She is always with me. We are side by side, close at hand, and *alongside* each other all the time. When two people are close in this way, they profoundly affect each other — even to the point where they begin to share the same attitudes, feelings, personality traits, habits, and gestures. In fact, they eventually know each other so well that they don't even have to ask what the other person is thinking — they already know.

The spiritual mentor-disciple relationship Paul and Timothy shared was probably similar in certain ways to the kind of close relationship I just described. Paul and Timothy had walked together for many years, spreading the message of the Gospel throughout the Roman world. To some degree, Timothy no doubt had picked up some of Paul's gestures, mannerisms, and thoughts, and he probably even sounded a little like Paul when he preached. The close relationship they shared allowed the truths of Paul's life to be transferred into Timothy. That is a natural consequence of this kind of intimacy.

This level of closeness is exactly what the word *para* refers to where it is used to form the compound word *parakletos*, or "Comforter," in John 14:16 and the other three references listed previously. Thus, we see that the Holy Spirit is close by and *alongside* each of us at all times. His relationship with us is not a distant one that requires us to beg and plead for Him to draw near. He is always with us. Doesn't the knowledge of that truth give you a greater level of peace in your heart and mind than you had before you understood it?

The Holy Spirit comes to reside inside us at the very moment we receive our salvation. However, this is not the full story. The use of the word *para* in John 14:16 reveals that He also comes *alongside* us to assist us in our daily affairs and to bring the reality of Jesus Christ into our lives. From the moment the Holy Spirit takes up residence in our hearts, we can continuously rely on His partnership to help us overcome any obstacles we might face in life.

In other words, when you accept Jesus as your Lord and Savior, the Holy Spirit comes into your life to provide you with the assistance Jesus would offer if He was present in the flesh. Whatever Jesus would do to assist you, that is precisely what the Holy Spirit will do. And didn't Jesus say, "…My peace I give unto you: not as the world giveth, give I unto you. Let not your heart be troubled, neither let it be afraid" (John 14:27)? Providing you with the assistance Jesus gave people when He was physically present on the earth is the Holy Spirit's ministry, and He is faithfully fulfilling that ministry today!

The Holy Spirit dwells in you as a permanent Resident and as the most reliable Partner you'll ever have in this life. That is why some newer versions of the New Testament translate the word "Comforter" as "Standby." In fact, the word "Standby" perfectly describes the Holy Spirit's close, side-by-side position in you from which He helps, empowers, guides, comforts, and gives you peace every step of the way.

There is no doubt that this word *para* describes the "*alongside* ministry" of the Holy Spirit.

Perhaps you were raised in a wonderful Bible-teaching church just as I was, but you have never experienced this kind of intimate relationship with the Holy

Spirit that I am describing to you. If not, today would be a great time to lift your hands and declare, "Holy Spirit, I receive You as my side-by-side Partner!" Then get ready for a divine adventure that never stops as He takes you to deeper levels of peace in Him!

My Prayer for Today

Holy Spirit, I know You live inside me, but I'm understanding afresh and anew that You are also side by side with me as my Partner in life. I have treated you like an invisible Guest, when, in reality, You have been sent to me to be at my side as my Helper and Standby in times of need. Please forgive me for overlooking and ignoring You when You have been waiting so long to assist me in life. Today I throw open my arms and my heart, and I say, "Welcome, Holy Spirit — I receive You as my side-by-side Partner who has been 'called alongside' in my life!"

I pray this in Jesus' name!

My Confession for Today

I confess that from this moment onward, I am wide open to the ministry of the Holy Spirit. Jesus sent the Spirit to be my Helper, and I certainly need His help. I will no longer ignore Him or disregard His presence in my life. I open my heart, mind, and soul to His peace-giving ministry. I will endeavor to recognize His voice, His leading, and His guidance, and I will strive to receive His supernatural help.

I declare this by faith in Jesus' name!

Questions for You To Consider

1. Of course the Holy Spirit lives inside you! But have you experienced moments when it was real to you that He was *right alongside you* — side by side — assisting you in decisions and actions that you needed to take? In what ways do you need to cooperate with Him more?

   _____

   _____

   _____

   _____

   _____

   _____

2. What were some of the instances in which you really experienced the "Standby" ministry of the Holy Spirit? Have you ever recalled those moments or shared them with someone else? Take a few minutes to tell a friend how you've experienced the comforting, peace-giving, helping ministry of the Spirit in your life.

   _____

   _____

   _____

   _____

   _____

   _____

3. After reading today's entry, what are you going to do differently to embrace the "alongside ministry" of the Holy Spirit in your life? In what area of your life do you most recognize the need for His help?

_____

_____

_____

_____

_____

About the Author

Rick Renner is a highly respected Bible teacher and leader in the international Christian community. He is the author of a long list of books, including the bestsellers *Dressed To Kill* and *Sparkling Gems From the Greek 1* and *2*, which have sold millions of copies in multiple languages worldwide. Rick's understanding of the Greek language and biblical history opens up the Scriptures in a unique way that enables his audience to gain wisdom and insight while learning something brand new from the Word of God. Rick and his wife Denise have cumulatively authored more than 40 books that have been distributed worldwide.

Rick is the overseer of the Good News Association of Churches, founder of the Moscow Good News Church, pastor of the Internet Good News Church, and founder of Media Mir. He is the president of GNC (Good News Channel) — the largest Russian-speaking Christian satellite network in the world, which broadcasts the Gospel 24/7 to countless Russian- and Ukrainian-speaking viewers worldwide via multiple satellites and the Internet. Rick is the founder of RENNER Ministries in Broken Arrow, Oklahoma, and host to his TV program, also seen around the world in multiple languages. Rick leads this amazing work with Denise — his wife and lifelong ministry partner — along with their sons and committed leadership team.

Equipping Believers to Walk in the Abundant Life

John 10:10b

Connect with us for fresh content and news about forthcoming books from your favorite authors...

 Facebook @ HarrisonHousePublishers

 Instagram @ HarrisonHousePublishing

 www.harrisonhouse.com